THE JOURNEY OF ARTIFICIAL INTELLIGENCE

Table of Contents

Introduction

Why focus on the history and future of Artificial Intelligence (AI)? Understanding the past helps us appreciate the present and anticipate the future. The history of AI is a testament to human innovation and the relentless pursuit of understanding intelligence. By studying its roots, we uncover the ideas and breakthroughs that laid the foundation for today's advancements.

The future of AI, on the other hand, holds immense potential. It's a future where machines could revolutionize industries, enhance our capabilities, and even redefine what it means to be human. But with great power comes responsibility. As AI continues to evolve, it presents challenges and ethical questions that we must address. This book aims to equip you with the knowledge to navigate these waters, making informed decisions about AI's role in our world.

Our journey begins with an overview of AI, defining what it is and why it matters. This section sets the stage, providing a clear understanding of AI's significance in today's world.

Next, we delve into the origins of AI. We'll explore early mechanical inventions, the pivotal contributions of Alan Turing, and the landmark 1956 Dartmouth Conference that marked AI's formal beginning. This historical perspective reveals the vision and ambition that have driven AI research for decades.

From there, we move into the early days of AI, focusing on symbolic AI and groundbreaking programs like the Logic Theorist and General Problem Solver. We'll also discuss the phenomenon known as the "AI Winter," periods when enthusiasm and funding waned, only to be rekindled by new advancements.

As we progress, we'll explore the rise of machine learning, highlighting the shift from rule-based systems to statistical models. This section covers key algorithms and techniques, showcasing how AI began to learn from data, leading to significant successes across various fields.

The big data revolution follows, emphasizing how large datasets have transformed AI applications. We'll examine technological advancements in storage and processing power and present case studies from industries like healthcare and retail that have harnessed AI's potential.

Deep learning and neural networks take center stage next. We'll explore the basics and key innovations of these technologies, highlighting their impact across diverse industries, from healthcare to finance.

We'll then turn our attention to current trends and breakthroughs in AI, covering natural language processing and robotics, among other areas. This section also addresses the ethical considerations surrounding AI, emphasizing the importance of responsible development.

Finally, we look towards the future, exploring emerging AI technologies and their potential societal impacts. From quantum machine learning to privacy-preserving techniques, we'll discuss expert predictions and the challenges we must overcome to harness AI's full potential.

"The Journey of Artificial Intelligence" is more than just a book about technology; it's a guide to understanding one of the most transformative forces of our time. By exploring AI's past, present, and future, we hope to inspire curiosity, foster understanding, and encourage thoughtful engagement with the world of AI.

Overview of AI: Define AI and Its Significance

Artificial Intelligence (AI) is a term that we often hear in today's world, but what does it actually mean? AI refers to the capability of machines to imitate intelligent human behavior. This means that AI systems can perform tasks that typically require human intelligence, such as understanding natural language, recognizing patterns, solving problems, and making decisions.

AI is not just about robots or automation; it includes software programs and applications that can perform tasks that typically require human intelligence; it is very much a part of our daily lives. From voice assistants like Siri and Alexa to recommendation systems on platforms like Netflix and Amazon, AI is shaping how we interact with technology. It can be categorized into two main types: Narrow AI and General AI.

1. **Narrow AI:** Also known as weak AI, this type is designed to perform a specific task. For example, AI used in chatbots, image recognition systems, and even online customer service assistance all fall under Narrow AI. These systems excel in their designated tasks but do not possess the ability to perform beyond them.

2. **General AI:** Often referred to as strong AI, this type would have the ability to understand, learn, and apply intelligence across a wide range of tasks, similar to a human being. However, General AI is still largely theoretical and has not yet been achieved.

AI holds great significance in various fields, including healthcare, finance, transportation, and education. Here are some of the ways AI is making a difference:

1. **Healthcare**: AI algorithms can analyze medical images and assist doctors in diagnosing diseases more accurately and quickly. For instance, systems can identify tumors in X-rays and MRIs with impressive precision.
2. **Finance:** In the financial sector, AI helps in fraud detection by analyzing transaction patterns and flagging unusual activities. Automated trading systems can analyze market data in real-time to make quick buy or sell decisions.
3. **Transportation:** AI is driving innovation in transportation with the development of self-driving cars. These vehicles use AI to navigate roads, recognize obstacles, and make decisions without human intervention.
4. **Education:** AI tools can personalize learning experiences for students. They can assess individual learning styles and provide tailored content that helps students grasp concepts at their own pace.

FIELD	APPLICATION	BENEFITS
Healthcare	Medical imaging analysis	Improved diagnosis speed and accuracy
Finance	Fraud detection	Enhanced security in transactions
Transportation	Autonomous vehicles	Increased safety and efficiency
Education	Personalized learning platforms	Tailored education for individual needs

As we move forward in this book, we will explore the different dimensions of AI and how it continues to evolve. It is essential to recognize that while AI brings tremendous benefits, it also poses challenges that we need to address collectively. Understanding AI is the first step in navigating its complexities and harnessing its potential for good.

CHAPTER 1
The Origins of AI

Early Concepts: Research Early Mechanical Inventions

The journey of artificial intelligence (AI) is deeply rooted in the early mechanical inventions that laid the groundwork for modern technology. Long before computers and AI became household terms, inventors and thinkers were exploring the limits of machinery and automaton. Understanding these early mechanical inventions helps contextualize the advancements we see today in AI and robotics.

Mechanical inventions can be traced back to ancient civilizations, where the desire to simplify human tasks led to the creation of various devices. For example, the ancient Greeks designed simple machines such as the screw press and the water wheel, which utilized basic mechanical principles to perform functions efficiently.

One of the first known inventors was *Archimedes*, who lived in the 3rd century BCE. His inventions, including the **Archimedes screw**[1], were primarily aimed at moving water, demonstrating an early understanding of mechanics. Such inventions not only showcased human ingenuity but also set the stage for more complex devices in later centuries.

During the Middle Ages and the Renaissance, the concept of **automata** took shape. These were self-operating machines designed to mimic human or animal actions. In the 13th century, the Arab engineer *Ismail al-Jazari* created remarkable mechanical devices, including water clocks and automata that could play music or serve drinks[2]. His book, *"The Book of Knowledge of Ingenious Mechanical Devices,"* described 50 different machines, providing valuable insight into early engineering and automation[3].

The invention of the **mechanical calculator** by Blaise Pascal in 1642 also paved the way for computational devices. This early calculator could perform addition and subtraction, and although simple by today's standards, it highlighted the potential for machines to handle numerical tasks.

By the 18th century, the idea of automata became even more advanced. The French inventor *Jacques de Vaucanson* created impressive mechanical figures that could play musical instruments and perform simple tasks. These early automata were powered by intricate systems of gears and levers, demonstrating the potential of machinery to replicate certain human actions.

The Industrial Revolution, which began in the late 18th century, marked a big turning point in mechanical invention. The development of **steam engines**[4] and **power looms**[5] revolutionized production processes and set the foundation for modern engineering. As the years progressed, thinkers like *George Boole* and *Gottfried Wilhelm Leibniz* began to theorize about the possibilities of machinery in processing information. Boole's work on **Boolean algebra** provided a framework for logical reasoning[6], while Leibniz envisioned a **universal language of symbols** that could represent ideas and actions[7]. These concepts were foundational for later developments in computing and artificial intelligence.

Early Mechanical Inventions

1. **The Antikythera Mechanism (circa 150-100 BC)**: Discovered in a shipwreck off the coast of Antikythera, Greece, this ancient device is considered the world's first analog computer. It was used to predict astronomical positions and eclipses for calendar and astrological purposes. The Antikythera Mechanism demonstrated an early understanding of gears and complex calculations, laying the groundwork for future mechanical inventions[8].

2. **Hero's Engine (circa 10-70 AD)**: Invented by Hero of Alexandria, this steam-powered device used steam pressure to create motion. It could spin around and was essentially the first example of a steam engine. Though it was never used for practical purposes, Hero's Engine showcased the potential of harnessing energy to create movement, a fundamental concept in mechanics that would eventually contribute to the development of machines, paving the way for more complex automation[9].

3. **Automata (circa 400 BC - 200 AD)**: Ancient civilizations, including the Greeks and Egyptians, created automata—self-operating machines that mimicked human and animal actions. For example, the ancient Greek engineer Ctesibius built machines that could play music or pour water. These creations were early explorations into making machines that could perform tasks autonomously, a concept that is central to modern AI development[3].

4. **The Mechanical Clock (13th Century)**: As societies became more structured and required precise timekeeping, the mechanical clock emerged. It represented a significant advancement in mechanics, combining gears, weights, and pendulums. By measuring time accurately, mechanical

clocks allowed for better organization in daily life and laid the groundwork for understanding systematic processes—an essential aspect of programming in AI[10].

5. **The Jacquard Loom (1804)**: This weaving machine, invented by Joseph Marie Jacquard, used punched cards to control the movement of the threads. The Jacquard Loom is crucial in the history of computing because it demonstrated how instructions could be encoded on a medium, allowing machines to operate autonomously based on predefined patterns. This concept of programming would later be foundational for computer programming and AI[11].

6. **Charles Babbage's Analytical Engine (1837)**: Often dubbed the first concept of a general-purpose computer, Babbage's design included features like a control unit, an arithmetic logic unit, and memory. Although it was never completed in his lifetime, the Analytical Engine introduced the idea of a programmable machine capable of performing any calculation, leading to thoughts about machine intelligence[12].

YEAR/PERIOD	INVENTION	INVENTOR/ REGION	SIGNIFICANCE
Circa 150-100 BC	Antikythera Mechanism	Greece	First analog computer for astronomical predictions.
Circa 10 AD	Hero's Engine	Alexandria	Early steam-powered device showcasing mechanical energy.	
Circa 400 BC - 200 AD	Automata	Greece/Egypt	Self-operating machines mimicking actions.
13th Century	Mechanical Clock	Europe	Precise timekeeping led to systematic processes.
1804	Jacquard Loom	France	Pioneered the concept of programming using punched cards.
1837	Analytical Engine	England	First concept of a general-purpose computer.

These early inventions did not exist in a vacuum; they built upon one another, creating a foundation for future technological advancements. Each invention contributed to a collective understanding of mechanics, automation, and the principles of programming. The quest to create machines that

11

can perform tasks without human intervention began with these early mechanical inventions, setting the stage for the eventual rise of artificial intelligence.

Turing and the Birth of AI

Born on June 23, 1912, in London, *Alan Mathison Turing* showed early signs of brilliance in mathematics and logic. His most notable contributions came during and after World War II, where his work on code-breaking and computing opened new avenues in technology[13].

One of Turing's primary contributions was the development of the concept of a *"universal machine,"* which is now known as the Turing Machine[13]. This theoretical machine could simulate any algorithm, acting as a foundation for modern computers. By defining this model, Turing demonstrated that a single machine could perform any computation given the right input and sufficient time. This idea was revolutionary as it showed that machines could be programmed to perform complex tasks.

Turing's work extended beyond theoretical concepts. He also helps during World War II at Bletchley Park, where he led efforts to break the German Enigma code. His success in deciphering encrypted messages not only contributed significantly to the Allied victory but also showcased the potential of machines in solving complex problems.

In 1950, Turing published a seminal paper titled **"Computing Machinery and Intelligence,"** where he posed a fundamental question: *"Can machines think?"* Turing believed that this question should be approached differently[14]. Instead of getting lost in the philosophical definitions of *"thinking,"* he proposed a practical test to evaluate a machine's ability to exhibit intelligent behavior. This became known as the **Turing Test**.

The Turing Test involves a human evaluator who interacts with both a machine and a human through a computer interface. The evaluator's task is to determine which participant is the machine and which is the human based solely on their responses to questions. If the evaluator cannot reliably tell the difference between the two, the machine is said to have passed the Turing Test[15].

The Turing Test is structured around three main participants:

1. **The Interrogator:** This is the human evaluator who poses questions to both the machine and the human. The interrogator's role is to gather information through conversation.

2. **The Human Respondent (foil):** This participant is tasked with providing human-like responses to the interrogator's questions, ensuring that they do not give away their identity as a human.

3. **The Machine Respondent:** This is the AI system or machine that is designed to respond in a way that mimics human conversation. Its goal is to mislead the interrogator into believing it is the human.

The Turing Test serves several purposes:

1. **Measuring Intelligence:** It provides a straightforward method for assessing whether a machine can demonstrate intelligent behavior comparable to a human.

2. **Defining AI:** The test helps to establish criteria for what constitutes artificial intelligence. If a machine can convincingly imitate human responses, it suggests a level of intelligence that warrants further exploration.

3. **Encouraging Development:** By providing a benchmark, the Turing Test inspires researchers and developers to create more sophisticated AI systems that can engage in meaningful conversation.

While the Turing Test is influential, it has its limitations:

1. **Surface-Level Interaction:** The test focuses primarily on conversational ability rather than understanding. A machine might pass the test without possessing true comprehension of the conversation.

2. **Contextual Understanding:** The Turing Test doesn't account for the depth of understanding or emotional intelligence. A machine might mimic human responses without grasping the underlying context or emotional nuances.

3. **Evaluator Bias:** The outcome can depend heavily on the evaluator's subjective judgment. Different evaluators might have varying standards for what constitutes human-like behavior.

Despite its limitations, the Turing Test has had a profound impact on the field of artificial intelligence. It has sparked debates about the nature of intelligence and raised important questions about the capabilities of machines. The concept continues to influence research and development in AI, encouraging innovative technologies aimed at improving human-computer interactions.

Over the years, various programs and chatbots have attempted to pass the Turing Test. One notable example is the chatbot *"ELIZA,"* created in the 1960s by Joseph Weizenbaum. ELIZA could simulate conversation by using keyword recognition and pattern matching. Although it impressed many, it ultimately failed to pass in more rigorous evaluations.

AI PROGRAM	YEAR CREATED	OUTCOME
ELIZA	1966	Failed to consistently pass
PARRY	1972	Passed in limited trials
ALICE	2000	Won Loebner Prize (2000)
Eugene Goostman	2014	Claimed to pass

The Turing Test continues to spark debates in both AI research and philosophy. As computers become more advanced, the question of what it means to think and understand remains relevant. Turing's ideas shifted the focus from trying to define intelligence to simply observing behavior. This approach allowed for a more practical framework for developing intelligent machines. In many ways, the Turing Test set the stage for future work in AI by establishing a method for evaluating machine intelligence.

After Turing's death in 1954, his contributions continued to influence the fields of computer science and artificial intelligence. Despite the challenges in creating machines that could fully replicate human thought, Turing's vision sparked a movement that has evolved into today's rapidly advancing AI technologies. His work has inspired and guided researchers, leading to the development of various AI applications that we encounter in our daily lives, from virtual assistants to recommendation algorithms.

The 1956 Dartmouth Conference and the Birth of AI as a Field

In the summer of 1956, a pivotal event took place that would lay the groundwork for what we now know as Artificial Intelligence (AI). This event was the Dartmouth Conference, held at Dartmouth College in Hanover, New Hampshire. Organized by John McCarthy, Marvin Minsky, Nathaniel Rochester, and Claude Shannon, the conference brought together some of the brightest minds in computer science, mathematics, and cognitive psychology[16]. Their goal? To explore the potential of machines to simulate aspects of human intelligence.

The idea of creating intelligent machines was not new, but the Dartmouth Conference marked the first formal gathering dedicated to this concept. The participants believed that if machines could be made to think and learn like humans, the implications would be profound—not just for technology, but for society as a whole. They aimed to define the field of AI and set the stage for future research.

The Dartmouth Conference featured several key figures, each contributing their unique insights.

1. **John McCarthy**: John McCarthy was one of the primary organizers of the Dartmouth Conference. He coined the term *"artificial intelligence"* during the conference, marking a significant moment in the field. He believed that human intelligence could be replicated in machines through programming.

Throughout his career, McCarthy developed the LISP programming language, which became one of the most widely used languages for AI research. His contributions laid the groundwork for future exploration in the field[17].

2. **Marvin Minsky**: Marvin Minsky was a cognitive scientist and a co-founder of the MIT Artificial Intelligence Laboratory. Minsky's work focused on understanding human thought processes, and he was deeply interested in how machines could replicate this behavior.

He believed that a machine could learn and adapt like a human, a concept that would later be fundamental to AI development. Minsky authored several influential books and papers on AI, further establishing his reputation as a leading thinker in the field[18].

3. **Nathaniel Rochester**: Nathaniel Rochester was a computer scientist at IBM and played a significant role in the organization of the Dartmouth Conference. He presented a paper during the conference that outlined how machines could be programmed to perform tasks that typically require human intelligence.

Rochester's work in machine learning and pattern recognition helped shape the early discussions at the conference. He later contributed to several AI projects at IBM, including the development of systems that could learn from data[19].

4. **Claude Shannon**: Claude Shannon, known as the father of information theory, was another influential figure in the AI community. Although he did not attend the Dartmouth Conference, his work laid the groundwork for many AI concepts.

Shannon's theories on data transmission and processing helped researchers understand how machines could manipulate information. His ideas on machine learning and communication have influenced AI development and continue to be relevant today[20].

During the two-month-long conference, participants engaged in discussions that ranged from theoretical frameworks to practical applications. They debated the capabilities of machines and what it would take to make them intelligent. A central theme was the idea that human problem-solving could be replicated through programming. The conference tackled several key questions:

- Can machines think?
- What types of problems could machines solve?
- What would be the best approach to creating intelligent machines?

These discussions led to a consensus that AI could be achieved through mathematical models and computational techniques. The participants believed that, within a few years, machines could be developed to perform tasks previously thought to require human intelligence.

The Dartmouth Conference ultimately produced a series of proposals for research projects aimed at advancing the field of AI. Some of the key outcomes included:

1. The establishment of a research agenda focused on areas such as reasoning, learning, and problem-solving.
2. Development of programming languages designed to facilitate AI research.

3. Creation of interdisciplinary teams combining knowledge from computer science, psychology, and neuroscience.

The event also served to inspire future generations of researchers and thinkers. It marked the beginning of a new academic field, one that would attract talent and funding over the decades to come. In the years following the conference, various projects emerged, including the development of early AI programs like the **Logic Theorist** and **General Problem Solver**. These projects showcased machines' ability to solve problems and perform tasks that had previously been thought to require human intelligence.

The impact of the Dartmouth Conference extended beyond the academic world. It attracted attention from government agencies and industries interested in leveraging AI for various applications. As a result, funding for AI research began to increase, leading to further advancements in the field.

The Dartmouth Conference was more than just a gathering of brilliant minds; it was a catalyst for a movement. It helped to formalize the idea of AI as an academic discipline and inspired countless researchers to explore the possibilities of machine intelligence. The discussions held in that summer of 1956 continue to influence the trajectory of AI today, reminding us that the dream of creating intelligent machines began with a simple gathering of ideas and aspirations.

CHAPTER 2
The Early Days

Symbolic AI and Early Programs

The Dartmouth Conference in 1956 officially launched AI as a field of study, and it set the stage for the development of what we now call Symbolic AI. **Symbolic AI** focuses on the manipulation of symbols, which represent concepts and relationships in a structured way. It differs from other approaches that rely on numerical data or statistical methods. Researchers believed that by representing knowledge in a form that computers could manipulate, they could replicate human reasoning and problem-solving abilities.

After the Dartmouth Conference, several early AI programs emerged that embodied the principles of Symbolic AI. These programs were groundbreaking for their time and laid the foundation for future developments in AI. Here are some notable ones:

Logic Theorist (1956)

In 1956, a groundbreaking program called the Logic Theorist was developed, created by Allen Newell and Herbert A. Simon at the RAND Corporation, this program was one of the first to demonstrate that machines could perform tasks that were typically associated with human reasoning. The Logic Theorist aimed to prove mathematical theorems by using a set of rules and logical operations, which laid the foundation for further advancements in AI[21].

The Logic Theorist was designed to solve problems in propositional logic. It could take a theorem from a mathematical text and find a proof for it, which was quite a remarkable achievement at the time. The program was capable of working through theorems from a logic book known as *"Principia Mathematica,"* authored by Alfred North Whitehead and Bertrand Russell[22]. This book comprised complex logical statements, and the Logic Theorist was able to prove 38 out of the first 52 theorems presented in it.

The operation of the Logic Theorist was based on a series of methods and procedures that closely resembled human thought processes. Here's how it functioned:

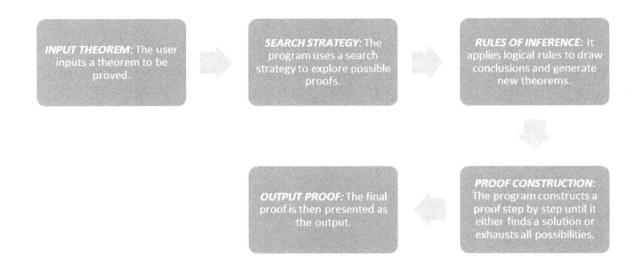

The Logic Theorist's successful demonstration of theorem proving marked a turning point in artificial intelligence research. It opened the door to further exploration of machine learning, natural language processing, and cognitive computing. Following its development, researchers began to realize the potential of AI systems in various fields beyond mathematics.

The Logic Theorist was also presented at the Dartmouth Conference in 1956, which is widely regarded as the birth of artificial intelligence as a field. This conference brought together some of the brightest minds of the time, and discussions from this event laid the groundwork for future developments in AI.

The Logic Theorist had a lasting influence on computational logic and the way we understand automated reasoning today. Its methods for proof generation and symbolic reasoning have been foundational in the development of more advanced AI systems. Many modern AI techniques, including theorem provers and automated reasoning systems, owe their origins to the concepts introduced by the Logic Theorist.

General Problem Solver (GPS, 1957)

Also created by Newell and Simon in 1957 at the RAND Corporation, the GPS aimed to solve a broad range of problems, not just mathematical ones. The General Problem Solver was created as a computer program that aimed to solve a variety of problems presented in a structured manner. It was built on the idea that human intelligence could be replicated by machines, allowing computers to tackle complex issues through a series of logical steps[23].

The developers aimed to create a system that could apply a general method to solve problems across different domains, rather than being restricted to a specific type of task. GPS operates based on a set of rules and procedures that guide it in solving problems. Here's a breakdown of its process:

1. **Problem Definition:** The user defines the problem clearly. This involves identifying the initial state (where you are) and the goal state (where you want to be).
2. **Means-Ends Analysis:** GPS employs a method called means-ends analysis. This means it continuously evaluates the difference between the current state and the goal state, identifying the steps needed to bridge that gap.
3. **Search and Solution:** The program explores possible actions or moves that can reduce the difference. It generates potential solutions and evaluates them against the predefined criteria until it finds a satisfactory answer.
4. **Execution of the Solution:** Once it identifies a solution, GPS can execute the steps required to achieve the goal state.

GPS was capable of solving simple mathematical problems and puzzles. For example, it could effectively tackle problems like the *Towers of Hanoi* or certain logic puzzles. Its ability to break down complex problems into manageable segments marked a significant advancement in the field of artificial intelligence.

However, GPS also had limitations. While it could solve specific problems with relative ease, it struggled with more complex or ill-defined problems. The reliance on well-structured representations meant that GPS was not as flexible as human problem-solving capabilities. It often required problems to be defined in a way that fit its rigid structure, which was not always possible.

Despite its limitations, GPS had a profound impact on the field of artificial intelligence. It opened the door for further research into problem-solving systems and laid the groundwork for future AI developments. The lessons learned from GPS about structured problem representation and search strategies continue to influence AI research today.

Moreover, GPS highlighted the importance of representation in AI. It spurred further research into how problems could be represented and how these representations could impact the efficacy of problem-solving algorithms. This has led to the development of various AI techniques, including heuristic search and optimization strategies that are widely used today.

LISP (1958)

LISP, which stands for List Processing, is one of the oldest programming languages still in use today. Developed in 1958 by John McCarthy at the Massachusetts Institute of Technology (MIT), LISP was created specifically for AI research. Its innovative features and adaptability made it the go-to language for AI projects over the decades.

John McCarthy wanted a language that could efficiently process symbolic information, making it particularly suited for AI applications. Before LISP, most programming was done in assembly language or early high-level languages like *Fortran*. McCarthy designed LISP with a focus on manipulating symbols rather than just numerical calculations. The first version of LISP was implemented on an IBM 704 computer, and it introduced several groundbreaking concepts that would shape programming languages for years to come[24].

Key Features of LISP

1. **Symbolic Expression (S-expressions):** LISP uses S-expressions to represent data and code uniformly. This means that the same notation is used to write both expressions and data, allowing for easier manipulation of code.
2. **Code as Data:** One of LISP's most powerful features is that code can be treated as data. This means that programs can manipulate themselves, enabling features like macros, which allow programmers to create new syntactic constructs in a straightforward way.
3. **Recursion:** LISP is one of the first programming languages to support recursion, a technique where a function calls itself to solve smaller instances of a problem. This approach is particularly useful in AI algorithms.
4. **Garbage Collection:** LISP introduced automatic memory management, known as garbage collection. This feature automatically reclaims memory that is no longer in use, helping to manage resources more efficiently.

5. **Dynamic Typing:** LISP is dynamically typed, meaning that variable types are determined at runtime. This flexibility allows for more rapid development and experimentation, which is essential in AI research.

LISP quickly became the favored language for AI research. Many early AI projects, including natural language processing, automated reasoning, and machine learning, were implemented in LISP. The language's ability to handle complex data structures and its support for symbolic reasoning made it ideal for these applications.

Throughout the years, several dialects of LISP have emerged, including Common LISP and Scheme. Each dialect has its own features and strengths, but the core concepts of LISP have remained influential.

Although other programming languages, such as *Python* and *Java*, have gained popularity in recent years, LISP has not disappeared. It is still used in specific AI applications, particularly in research and development. Its unique features continue to inspire new programming languages and paradigms.

ELIZA (1966)

Developed by Joseph Weizenbaum at the MIT Artificial Intelligence Laboratory, ELIZA was one of the first programs capable of engaging users in natural language conversation. ELIZA was a computer program designed to simulate conversation by using natural language processing. It did this by recognizing specific keywords and phrases from the user's input and generating responses based on pre-defined rules.

The most famous of ELIZA's implementations was the "DOCTOR" script, which mimicked a Rogerian psychotherapist. This meant that when users communicated with ELIZA, they felt as though they were speaking to a therapist who was there to listen and reflect their thoughts back to them.

ELIZA operated using a simple structure. It employed pattern matching to identify keywords in the user's input and then applied transformation rules to create responses. For instance, if a user said, "I am feeling sad," ELIZA might respond with, "Why do you feel sad?" This back-and-forth exchange created the illusion of a conversation, even though ELIZA did not understand the content of the dialogue in a human sense.

Here is a representation of how ELIZA's response generation worked:

```
Welcome to
         EEEEEE  LL     IIII  ZZZZZZ  AAAAA
         EE      LL      II       ZZ  AA  AA
         EEEEE   LL      II      ZZZ  AAAAAAA
         EE      LL      II      ZZ   AA  AA
         EEEEEE  LLLLLL IIII  ZZZZZZ  AA  AA

   Eliza is a mock Rogerian psychotherapist.
   The original program was described by Joseph Weizenbaum in 1966.
   This implementation by Norbert Landsteiner 2005.


ELIZA: Is something troubling you ?
YOU:   Men are all alike.
ELIZA: What is the connection, do you suppose ?
YOU:   They're always bugging us about something or other.
ELIZA: Can you think of a specific example ?
YOU:   Well, my boyfriend made me come here.
ELIZA: Is it important to you that your boyfriend made you come here ?
YOU:   He says I'm depressed much of the time.
ELIZA: I am sorry to hear that you are depressed.
YOU:   It's true. I am unhappy.
ELIZA: Can you explain what made you unhappy ?
YOU:
```

SOURCE: *https://en.wikipedia.org/wiki/ELIZA#/media/File:ELIZA_conversation.png*

One of the most fascinating aspects of ELIZA was the reaction it elicited from users. Many people began to attribute human-like qualities to the program. They felt a connection and often revealed personal thoughts and feelings during their interactions with ELIZA. This phenomenon surprised Weizenbaum himself, as he had not anticipated that users would become emotionally invested in a computer program.

Weizenbaum's work raised important questions about the nature of communication between humans and machines. He emphasized the ethical implications of creating systems that could mimic human interaction. This led to discussions on the limits of artificial intelligence and the potential emotional impact of these technologies on users.

Despite its simplicity, ELIZA showcased the potential of artificial intelligence in language and communication. The system was not perfect; ELIZA had significant limitations. It did not possess any real understanding of language or context.

While ELIZA did not pass the *Turing Test* in a strict sense, it did raise important questions about how users perceive intelligence in machines. Many users believed they were conversing with a human, demonstrating that the illusion of understanding is often enough to influence people's perceptions.

However, it's essential to note that while ELIZA could mimic conversation, it did not possess true understanding or reasoning skills. The program operated purely on patterns and keywords, lacking the depth of human thought.

Over the years, ELIZA's influence can be seen in numerous advancements in AI conversational agents. Modern chatbots and virtual assistants, like *Siri* and *Alexa*, owe a part of their development to early programs like ELIZA. While today's systems are far more sophisticated, the foundational concepts introduced by Weizenbaum remain relevant.

SHRDLU (1970)

Created by Terry Winograd in 1970 at the Massachusetts Institute of Technology (MIT), SHRDLU was designed to understand and manipulate blocks in a virtual environment using natural language. This program became a key milestone in the field of AI and natural language processing, demonstrating what machines could achieve when given the ability to comprehend human language.

The primary purpose of SHRDLU was to interact with users in plain English, allowing them to communicate with a computer program as easily as they would with another person. The program worked within a simplified world made up of blocks, where users could ask SHRDLU to manipulate these blocks based on commands like *"move the red block"* or *"pick up the blue block."* This interactive experience marked a significant step forward in the quest for machines that could understand human language[25].

SHRDLU utilized a combination of natural language understanding and problem-solving capabilities. It could parse sentences to identify relevant information, understand context, and execute commands based on the input it received. This was a groundbreaking development at the time, as earlier AI systems were limited to pre-defined commands and could not handle the complexities of human language effectively. Here are some key features of SHRDLU:

1. **Natural Language Input:** Users could interact with the program using English sentences.
2. **Contextual Understanding:** The program could maintain context over a series of commands.
3. **Object Manipulation:** SHRDLU could simulate the movement and interaction of blocks in a defined space.

4. **Semantic Understanding:** It was capable of recognizing synonyms and different phrasing for similar actions.

The architecture of SHRDLU was particularly notable for its ability to keep track of the state of the blocks and the actions taken by the user. For instance, if a user instructed SHRDLU to *"Move the blue block next to the green block,"* it would understand the current positions of all blocks, update their locations accordingly, and provide feedback. This level of interactivity showcased a significant leap forward in human-computer interaction.

Another essential aspect of SHRDLU was its ability to answer questions about the blocks world. Users could ask, *"Which blocks are on top of the green block?"* and SHRDLU would provide accurate, contextual responses based on its understanding of the virtual environment. This capability highlighted the potential for AI to act not just as a tool for executing commands, but as a conversational partner that could engage in meaningful dialogue.

Despite its advances, SHRDLU was not without limitations. It operated in a controlled environment with a limited vocabulary and a specific set of commands. As a result, it struggled with more complex language structures and real-world scenarios.

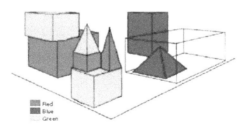

Person: Pick up a big red block.
Computer: OK.
Person: Grasp the pyramid.
Computer: I don't understand which pyramid you mean.

SOURCE: https://cryptlabs.com/understanding-shrdlu-a-pioneering-ai-in-language-and-reasoning/

However, its contributions laid the groundwork for future developments in natural language processing and artificial intelligence. By demonstrating that machines could understand and respond to human language in a meaningful way, it paved the way for further research in this field.

These early programs had a profound effect on the direction of AI research. They showcased the possibilities of using strictly symbolic approaches to solve problems that were previously thought to require human intelligence. The successes of these programs generated excitement in the AI community and spurred further research.

Despite their achievements, these programs also faced limitations. The complexity of human reasoning and understanding often proved challenging to replicate in machines. Nevertheless, the foundational work laid by these early AI programs fueled ongoing research and innovation, leading to new methodologies and technologies in the field.

The AI Winter: The Rise and Fall of Early AI Hype and Funding

By the 1950s and 1960s, AI gained significant attention. Early successes, including simple problem-solving programs and the development of neural networks, fueled optimism. Governments and private institutions invested heavily in AI research, seeing it as a path to unprecedented technological advancement.

The term **"AI Winter"** refers to periods when the artificial intelligence field faced reduced funding and waning interest. These winters were marked by cycles of heavy investment and enthusiasm, followed by disappointment, skepticism, and significant cutbacks in resources.

The first usage of **"AI Winter"** appeared in 1984 during a debate at the American Association of Artificial Intelligence (AAAI) annual meeting. Prominent AI researchers, Roger Schank and Marvin Minsky, cautioned that the excitement around AI in the 1980s was unsustainable and that a downturn was inevitable[26].

The First AI Winter (1974–1980)

The seeds of the first AI Winter were sown in the late 1960s and early 1970s. Several setbacks contributed to the decline in confidence and funding:

1. **1966 (Machine Translation Failures):** The dream of translating languages through machines fell short. The results were often inaccurate, leading to disappointment.

2. **1969 (Criticism of Perceptrons)**: Early artificial neural networks, known as perceptrons, were criticized for their limitations, particularly their inability to solve complex problems. This criticism contributed to the skepticism surrounding AI's potential.

3. **1973 (The Lighthill Report):** In the UK, the Lighthill Report criticized the lack of progress in AI research, leading to a significant cutback in funding.

4. **1973-1974: DARPA's Cutbacks**: In the United States, DARPA scaled back funding for AI research after being dissatisfied with the outcomes of several projects, including the Speech Understanding Research program at Carnegie Mellon University.

These factors collectively led to the first AI Winter, a period when the field struggled to maintain momentum.

The Second AI Winter (1987–2000)

The second wave of AI Winter began in the late 1980s. Despite the initial success of AI in business applications, the industry faced several challenges:

1. **1987 (Collapse of the LISP Machine Market)**: LISP machines, which were specialized for AI applications, became obsolete due to advances in general-purpose computers.

2. **1988 (Strategic Computing Initiative)**: New AI spending by the Strategic Computing Initiative was canceled, reflecting a broader loss of confidence.

3. **1990s (Abandonment of Expert Systems)**: Many expert systems, once hailed as the future of AI, were abandoned due to maintenance difficulties and the inability to adapt to new information.

4. **1990s (Fifth Generation Computer Project):** Japan's ambitious Fifth Generation project, aiming to create computers using massively parallel computing, failed to meet its original goals, leading to further disillusionment.

This second winter saw AI research retreat into academia, with less commercial interest and fewer practical applications. The AI Winters teach us important lessons about technological development and human expectations. They highlight the need for realistic goals and timelines in research. During periods of hype, it is easy to overlook the complexities and challenges inherent in developing advanced technologies.

Despite these setbacks, AI began to regain interest in the early 2000s. The key turning point came around 2012 with breakthroughs in machine learning, particularly deep learning. This renewed interest led to a surge in funding and corporate investment, setting the stage for the current AI boom.

Expert Systems (1980s): The Development and Impact

In the 1980s, the field of artificial intelligence saw a remarkable shift with the rise of expert systems. These computer programs were designed to mimic the decision-making ability of a human expert in specific domains. They emerged as an exciting application of AI technology, providing invaluable support in various industries, including medicine, finance, and manufacturing.

Expert systems are AI programs that use a set of rules to analyze information and solve problems. They consist of two main components: the **knowledge base** and the **inference engine**. The knowledge base contains domain-specific information—facts, rules, and relationships relevant to a particular field. The inference engine applies logical rules to the knowledge base to deduce new information or make decisions[27].

During the 1980s, expert systems gained significant attention for their ability to assist with complex tasks that typically required human expertise. They provided solutions in areas where human practitioners faced challenges due to the volume of data or the intricacies of the subject matter.

Several notable developments propelled the growth of expert systems during this decade:

1. **Commercialization:** The 1980s marked the commercialization of expert systems. Companies began to invest in these technologies, leading to the development of numerous products that catered to various industries. This commercial interest translated into job opportunities and a broader recognition of AI's potential.

2. **Increased Accessibility:** The introduction of user-friendly interfaces made expert systems more accessible to non-technical users. This accessibility expanded their reach into sectors that had previously been hesitant to adopt AI solutions.

3. **Education and Training:** Educational institutions began incorporating expert systems into their curriculum. Students learned about the principles of knowledge representation and reasoning, preparing a new generation of professionals skilled in AI technologies.

4. **Diverse Applications:** Expert systems found applications in various fields, including medicine, where they assisted doctors in diagnosing diseases. In finance, they helped traders make investment decisions by analyzing market data. In manufacturing, they optimized processes and improved quality control.

Several expert systems made significant impacts during the 1980s:

MYCIN

Developed at Stanford University in the early 1970s, MYCIN made a significant impact throughout the 1980s. It was created to diagnose bacterial infections and recommend antibiotics. MYCIN operated by asking the user a series of questions to gather information about the patient's symptoms and medical history. Based on the responses, MYCIN utilized its extensive database of medical knowledge to provide a diagnosis and treatment plan.

The system was notable for its ability to handle uncertainty. MYCIN could provide recommendations even when it lacked complete information, which was a considerable step forward in medical AI. Although it never made it into clinical practice due to ethical and legal concerns, MYCIN influenced many subsequent expert systems in the healthcare field[28].

DENDRAL

Another pioneering expert system, DENDRAL, was developed in the late 1960s but gained traction in the 1980s. DENDRAL was designed to assist chemists in identifying molecular structures from mass spectrometry data. It analyzed chemical compounds and suggested possible molecular structures by utilizing a set of rules derived from a vast database of chemical knowledge.

DENDRAL was particularly effective in handling complex organic compounds that would take human experts considerable time to analyze. This system not only demonstrated the potential of AI in chemistry but also laid the groundwork for more sophisticated systems in the future[29].

XCON (also known as R1)

Developed by Digital Equipment Corporation (DEC) in the early 1980s, XCON was designed to automate the configuration of computer systems. XCON helped engineers determine the appropriate components needed to fulfill customer orders for computer systems by analyzing customer requirements and selecting suitable hardware and software configurations.

XCON was highly successful and saved DEC considerable time and money. At its peak, the system processed thousands of orders daily, significantly reducing the workload for human engineers. This success showcased the practical benefits of expert systems in business and manufacturing processes[30].

PROSPECTOR

PROSPECTOR was an expert system used in the mining industry, developed at Stanford University. It was designed to assist geologists in mineral exploration by analyzing geological data and making recommendations about potential mining sites. PROSPECTOR used rules that incorporated geological knowledge and data from various sources.

This system was notable for its ability to integrate diverse types of information, such as geological maps and historical data. PROSPECTOR demonstrated how expert systems could enhance decision-making processes in resource management, leading to more efficient mining operations[31].

CADUCEUS

CADUCEUS was an expert system designed for medical diagnosis, developed in the 1980s. Unlike MYCIN, which focused primarily on infections, CADUCEUS aimed to diagnose a broader range of medical conditions. It employed a large knowledge base and could reason through complex symptoms to arrive at potential diagnoses.

Despite its advanced capabilities, CADUCEUS faced similar challenges as MYCIN in terms of acceptance within the medical community. Nevertheless, it further demonstrated the potential of AI in healthcare and influenced future systems aimed at improving patient care[32].

The rise of expert systems in the 1980s had a profound impact on various sectors:

1. **Efficiency:** They significantly increased efficiency by processing information quickly and providing consistent recommendations. This efficiency allowed professionals to focus on higher-level tasks rather than getting bogged down by routine decision-making.

2. **Decision-Making Support:** Expert systems acted as valuable decision-making aids. By providing evidence-based recommendations, they helped professionals make informed choices, reducing the risk of errors.

3. **Knowledge Preservation:** With the aging workforce in many industries, expert systems became crucial for preserving knowledge. They captured the expertise of seasoned professionals, ensuring that valuable insights were not lost as employees retired.

Despite their impact, expert systems also faced challenges in the 1980s. Knowledge acquisition proved to be a significant hurdle; gathering and formalizing expert knowledge was time-consuming and often met with resistance from those unwilling to share their insights. Additionally, many expert systems struggled with the complexity of real-world scenarios, leading to limitations in their effectiveness.

EXPERT SYSTEM	YEAR DEVELOPED	FIELD	KEY FUNCTIONALITY
MYCIN	1970s	Medicine	Diagnosis of bacterial infections and treatment advice
DENDRAL	Late 1960s	Chemistry	Identification of molecular structures
XCON (R1)	Early 1980s	Business	Configuration of computer systems
PROSPECTOR	1980s	Mining	Recommendations for mineral exploration
CADUCEUS	1980s	Medicine	Diagnosis of a wide range of medical conditions

CHAPTER 3
The Rise of Machine Learning

From Symbolic AI to Machine Learning: From Rule-Based Systems to Statistical Models

In the earlier days of AI, systems were primarily built on symbolic AI, which relied on predefined rules and logic to process information. These systems used human-like reasoning to make decisions based on a set of rules. For example, if a specific condition was met, then a particular action would follow. This approach worked well for problems with clear rules and definitions but faced significant challenges in more complex environments.

Symbolic AI required extensive knowledge engineering, which meant human experts needed to define all the rules and relationships within a domain. This process was time-consuming and often led to systems that struggled to handle unexpected situations or new data. As a result, symbolic AI became limited in its application and effectiveness.

As computer processing power increased and the volume of data available grew, researchers began to explore alternatives to rule-based systems. This led to the emergence of **machine learning**, a subset of AI that focuses on building systems that learn from data rather than relying solely on hard-coded rules.

Machine learning allows systems to identify patterns, make decisions, and improve over time without explicit programming. This capability is particularly useful in environments where rules are difficult to define or where data is abundant but unstructured. The shift from symbolic AI to machine learning marked a significant change in how we approach AI development.

To better understand the transition, let's look at the key differences between symbolic AI and machine learning:

FEATURE	SYMBOLIC AI	MACHINE LEARNING
Approach	Rule-based, logical reasoning	Data-driven, statistical modeling
Knowledge Representation	Explicitly defined rules	Patterns learned from data
Flexibility	Rigid, limited to predefined rules	Adaptive, improves with more data
Handling Uncertainty	Struggles with ambiguous data	Capable of managing uncertainty
Development Time	Lengthy; requires manual rules	Faster; relies on data availability

The transition from symbolic AI to machine learning did not happen overnight. It involved a gradual recognition of the need for more flexible systems. Researchers and practitioners began exploring methods for teaching machines to learn from examples rather than relying solely on coded rules. This shift was driven by several factors:

1. **Increased Data Availability:** With the rise of the internet and digital technologies, vast amounts of data became accessible. This influx of information provided the raw material needed to train machine learning models effectively.

2. **Advancements in Computing Power:** The development of more powerful processors and specialized hardware, such as graphics processing units (GPUs), made it feasible to run complex algorithms that could learn from data at scale.

3. **Improved Algorithms:** Over time, researchers developed more sophisticated algorithms that could effectively analyze data and improve over time. This progress enabled machines to perform tasks that were previously thought to be exclusive to humans.

4. **Real-World Needs:** Industries needed solutions that could adapt to changing conditions, handle uncertainty, and provide insights based on data. This demand propelled the adoption of machine learning techniques across various sectors.

Machine learning systems have several advantages over symbolic AI:

1. **Scalability:** Machine learning can easily scale to handle large datasets, allowing for the processing of vast amounts of information. This capability means that as more data becomes available, the model can adapt and refine its predictions or classifications.

2. **Flexibility:** Unlike symbolic AI, which relies on fixed rules, machine learning models can learn from new data and adjust their behavior accordingly. This adaptability makes them better suited for real-world applications where conditions frequently change.

3. **Pattern Recognition:** Machine learning excels at recognizing patterns and making predictions based on those patterns. This strength is beneficial in fields such as finance, healthcare, and marketing, where identifying trends can lead to better decision-making.

4. **Managing Uncertainty:** Machine learning techniques are designed to work with uncertainty and noise in data, making them more robust in situations where information is incomplete or ambiguous.

The transition from symbolic AI to machine learning marks a critical evolution in the field of artificial intelligence. While rule-based systems provided a foundational understanding of AI, the limitations of these approaches sparked the development of machine learning, which offers greater adaptability and powerful data-driven insights.

As we move forward in our exploration of AI, it's essential to recognize how this shift has influenced not only the technology but also the way we interact with and benefit from intelligent systems in our daily lives.

Key Algorithms and Techniques

The more data a machine learning model can access, the better it can learn patterns and make decisions. The algorithms used in machine learning can be broadly categorized into three main types: supervised learning, unsupervised learning, and reinforcement learning. Each of these types serves different purposes and utilizes various techniques for analysis.

Supervised Learning

Supervised learning is the most common type of machine learning. In this approach, we train a model using a labeled dataset, where each input comes with a corresponding output label. The goal is for the model to learn a mapping from inputs to outputs, enabling it to make predictions on new, unseen data[33].

1. **Linear Regression**: Linear regression works by establishing a relationship between the dependent variable (the outcome we want to predict) and one or more independent variables (the factors that influence the outcome). The goal is to find the best-fitting line that describes how the independent variables affect the dependent variable[34].

For example, if we want to predict house prices based on factors like square footage, number of bedrooms, and location, linear regression will analyze the data to find the equation of the line that best represents the relationship between these features and the price.

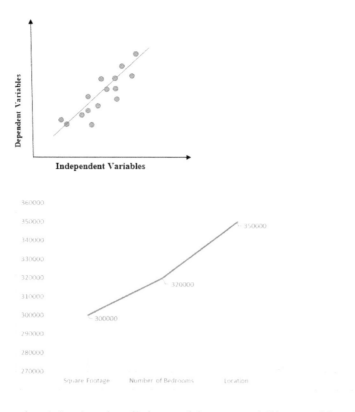

Linear regression is valued for its simplicity and interpretability, making it a popular choice for many applications.

2. **Logistic Regression**: While linear regression is used for predicting continuous outcomes, logistic regression is used for binary classification problems. This means it predicts outcomes that fall into one of two categories, such as "yes" or "no," "spam" or "not spam," and so on[35].

Logistic regression uses a logistic function to model the probabilities that an event occurs. The output is a value between 0 and 1, which indicates the likelihood of the dependent variable falling into a particular category. For instance, if we want to predict whether a student will pass or fail an exam based on their study hours, we can use logistic regression to analyze the data.

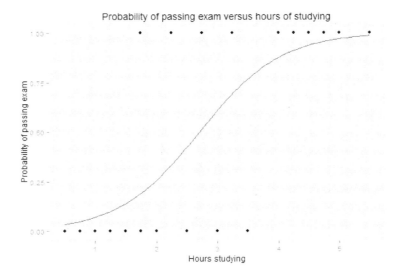

Probability of passing exam versus hours of studying

This algorithm is widely used in various fields, including healthcare, finance, and marketing, due to its effectiveness in binary classification tasks.

3. **Decision Trees**: Decision trees are another popular supervised learning algorithm that can be used for both classification and regression tasks. A decision tree is a flowchart-like structure where each internal node represents a decision based on the value of a feature, each branch represents the outcome of that decision, and each leaf node represents a final prediction[36].

For instance, if we want to predict whether a customer will buy a product based on their age and income, a decision tree would split the data at various nodes to make a series of yes-or-no decisions until reaching a conclusion.

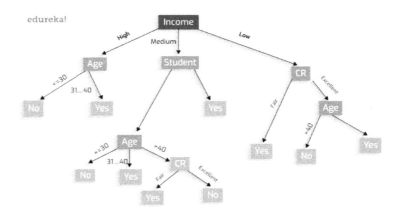

Decision trees are intuitive and easy to visualize, which makes them a great choice for interpreting complex data. However, they can become overly complex if not properly managed, leading to overfitting.

4. **Support Vector Machines (SVM)**: Support Vector Machines (SVM) are a powerful supervised learning algorithm primarily used for classification tasks. The core idea behind SVM is to find the optimal hyperplane that separates different classes in the data. A hyperplane is a flat affine subspace that provides a boundary between classes[37].

In cases where the classes are not linearly separable, SVM can use a technique called the **kernel trick**, allowing it to operate in a higher-dimensional space, making it easier to find a suitable hyperplane.

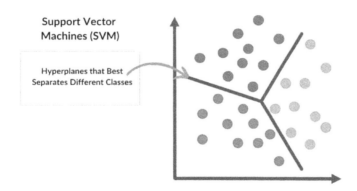

SVMs are known for their effectiveness in high-dimensional spaces and are widely used in applications such as image recognition and bioinformatics.

Unsupervised Learning

Unlike supervised learning, where algorithms learn from labeled data, unsupervised learning seeks to uncover hidden patterns in data without prior labeling. The goal here is to discover patterns or groupings within the data. These algorithms have paved the way for advancements in various fields, from marketing to healthcare[38].

K-Means Clustering

K-Means Clustering is one of the simplest and most widely used algorithms in unsupervised learning. The goal of K-Means is to partition a dataset into K distinct clusters based on feature similarity[39]. Here is how it works:

1. **Initialization:** Choose K initial centroids randomly from the dataset.
2. **Assignment:** For each data point, calculate its distance to each centroid and assign the point to the nearest centroid's cluster.
3. **Update:** After all points are assigned, recalculate the centroids as the mean of all points in each cluster.
4. **Repeat:** Repeat the assignment and update steps until the assignments no longer change significantly or a maximum number of iterations is reached.

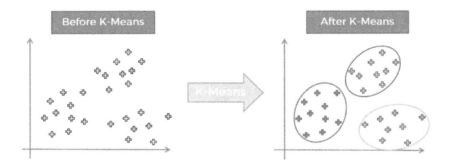

SOURCE: http://arun-aiml.blogspot.com/2017/07/k-means-clustering.html

This algorithm is efficient and works well for large datasets. However, it requires prior knowledge of the number of clusters (K), which can sometimes be a drawback. K-Means is particularly effective in customer segmentation, image compression, and market research.

Hierarchical Clustering

Hierarchical Clustering offers another approach to clustering that creates a tree-like structure, also known as a **dendrogram**. This algorithm can be divided into two main types: agglomerative (bottom-up) and divisive (top-bottom)[40].

1. **Agglomerative Clustering:** This is the most common approach. Starting with each data point as its own cluster, it iteratively merges the closest clusters until only one cluster remains or a

specified number of clusters is achieved. The closeness of clusters can be defined using different distance metrics, such as Euclidean or Manhattan distance.

2. **Divisive Clustering:** This approach starts with one single cluster containing all data points and progressively splits the cluster into smaller clusters.

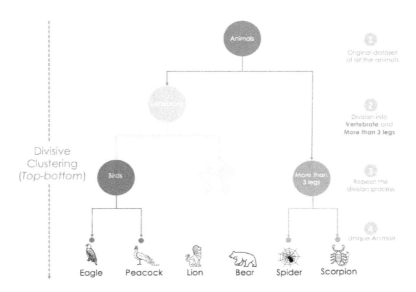

SOURCE: https://www.datacamp.com/tutorial/introduction-hierarchical-clustering-python

The Hierarchical Clustering lies create a hierarchy of clusters, which can provide insights into the data structure. It is widely used in fields such as biology for classifying species and in marketing to understand customer behavior.

Principal Component Analysis (PCA)

Principal Component Analysis (PCA) is another pivotal algorithm in unsupervised learning, primarily used for dimensionality reduction. It transforms a dataset into a set of orthogonal variables called principal components, which capture the most variance in the data[41]. Here's how PCA works:

1. **Standardization:** Normalize the dataset to have a mean of zero and a standard deviation of one to ensure that all features contribute equally.

2. **Covariance Matrix:** Calculate the covariance matrix to understand how different dimensions relate to each other.

3. **Eigenvalues and Eigenvectors:** Compute the eigenvalues and eigenvectors of the covariance matrix. The eigenvectors represent the directions of maximum variance, while the eigenvalues indicate their magnitude.

4. **Selecting Principal Components:** Choose the top K eigenvectors (principal components) that correspond to the largest eigenvalues. These eigenvectors form the new feature space.

5. **Transformation:** Project the original data onto this new feature space.

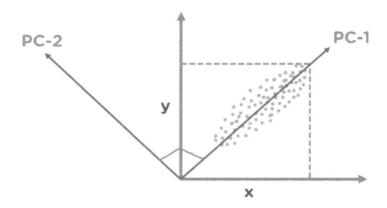

SOURCE: https://www.simplilearn.com/tutorials/machine-learning-tutorial/principal-component-analysis

PCA helps reduce the dimensionality of complex datasets, making it easier to visualize them in two or three dimensions. It is used in facial recognition systems to reduce the number of dimensions in image data while keeping the essential features. PCA can be also employed to identify patterns in stock prices and understand the underlying factors impacting market movements.

Reinforcement Learning

Reinforcement learning is a unique approach where an agent learns to make decisions by interacting with an environment to achieve a specific goal. The agent receives feedback in the form of rewards or penalties based on its actions. Over time, the agent aims to maximize the total reward it receives, essentially learning the best strategies for success[42].

In reinforcement learning, the process can be broken down into a few fundamental components:

1. **Agent:** The learner or decision-maker.

2. **Environment:** The external system that the agent interacts with.

3. **Actions:** The choices the agent can make.

4. **Rewards**: Feedback from the environment based on the agent's actions.

5. **Policy:** A strategy that the agent follows to determine its actions based on observations of the environment.

6. **Value Function:** A function that estimates the expected return or total reward for each state.

Reinforcement learning operates on the principle of trial and error. The agent tries different actions and learns from the outcomes. There are a few key concepts that drive this learning process.

1. **Exploration vs. Exploitation:** The agent faces a dilemma: should it explore new actions to discover potentially better rewards or exploit known actions that yield good rewards? Striking a balance between these two is essential for effective learning.

2. **Markov Decision Process (MDP):** Reinforcement learning often models decision-making problems using MDPs, where the outcome of an action depends not only on the current state but also on future states. MDPs provide a mathematical framework for analyzing the agent's interactions with the environment.

3. **Temporal Difference Learning:** This is a method where the agent learns from the differences between predicted rewards and actual rewards over time. It allows the agent to improve its policy based on new information.

Reinforcement learning has a wide array of applications across various domains. Here are some notable examples:

1. **Gaming:** RL has achieved remarkable success in gaming. For instance, DeepMind's AlphaGo used reinforcement learning to defeat human champions in the board game Go. The AI learned optimal strategies through countless games against itself, showcasing how RL can outperform human intuition.

2. **Robotics:** In robotics, RL is used to teach robots how to perform tasks, such as walking or grasping objects. Through trial and error, robots learn movements that maximize their effectiveness and efficiency in real-world scenarios.

3. **Healthcare:** In the healthcare sector, RL can optimize treatment plans for patients. For example, it can help in personalizing medication dosages based on individual responses, improving patient outcomes.

4. **Finance:** In financial markets, RL algorithms can be used for trading strategies. They analyze historical data and adjust trading actions in real-time to maximize returns while minimizing risks.

5. **Marketing:** Companies use RL to improve customer engagement. By analyzing user interactions, businesses can tailor their marketing strategies in real-time, ensuring that advertisements are more relevant and effective.

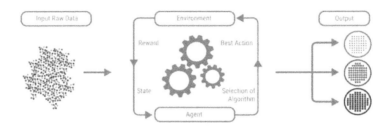

SOURCE: https://rancholabs.medium.com/reinforcement-learning-in-ai-ce979dc62fc3

Reinforcement learning is still a developing field, and its potential is immense. As computational power increases and algorithms become more sophisticated, we can expect to see more advanced applications in areas such as autonomous systems, smart cities, and personalized user experiences. However, challenges remain. Issues such as sample efficiency (the amount of data needed to learn effectively) and safety (ensuring that the agent does not take harmful actions) are areas of ongoing research.

As technology advances, reinforcement learning is expected to play a larger role in artificial intelligence. Innovations in algorithms, combined with increased computational power, will allow for more sophisticated RL applications. We can anticipate improvements in efficiency, safety, and scalability.

Neural Networks

The concept of neural networks can be traced back to the 1940s when psychologists and computer scientists began to study how the human brain processes information. In 1943, Warren McCulloch and Walter Pitts published a paper proposing a simplified model of the brain's neurons. They described how neurons could be represented as binary units that could be activated or deactivated based on inputs. This groundbreaking work laid the foundation for the first artificial neurons, known as **perceptrons**[43].

In 1957, Frank Rosenblatt introduced the perceptron, an early type of neural network. The perceptron could learn to classify inputs by adjusting its weights based on errors in its predictions. This was a significant step forward in machine learning, as it demonstrated that machines could be trained to recognize patterns. However, the perceptron had limitations. It could only solve linearly separable problems, which restricted its effectiveness in more complex scenarios.

Despite the initial excitement around neural networks, interest waned in the 1960s and 1970s. Researchers faced challenges in training multi-layer networks, and the limitations of the perceptron became apparent. The publication of Marvin Minsky and Seymour Papert's book, "Perceptrons," in 1969, highlighted these shortcomings and led to a decline in funding and research in the field. This period became known as the "AI winter," a time when enthusiasm for artificial intelligence cooled significantly.

The resurgence of neural networks began in the 1980s with the introduction of the **backpropagation algorithm**. This method allowed for the training of multi-layer neural networks, overcoming some of the limitations of the perceptron. Researchers such as Geoffrey Hinton, David Parker, and Yann LeCun played key roles in this revival. The backpropagation algorithm adjusted the weights of connections in a neural network through a systematic process, making it possible to minimize error and improve predictions.

This new wave of interest led to a variety of applications, from image recognition to speech processing. Despite its potential, the technology was still limited by the computational power available at the time. Training large networks required significant resources, and as such, progress was gradual.

By the 1980s, the introduction of hidden layers transformed neural networks into more capable systems known as **Multi-Layer Perceptrons (MLPs).** These networks could learn complex, non-linear mappings from input to output, opening doors to a variety of applications that were previously unattainable[44].

In 1985, Geoffrey Hinton introduced **Boltzmann Machines**, a type of stochastic neural network that employed a probabilistic approach to learning. This innovation marked a step forward in understanding and harnessing neural networks' potential, as it brought new ways to tackle AI problems.

As computational power improved, so did the capabilities of neural networks. The 1990s saw the emergence of more sophisticated architectures, such as **convolutional neural networks** (CNNs) and **recurrent neural networks** (RNNs). CNNs, developed for image processing tasks, allowed for the extraction of features from visual data more effectively. RNNs, on the other hand, were designed to handle sequential data, making them ideal for tasks like language modeling and time series prediction.

During this period, researchers also began to explore unsupervised learning techniques, where neural networks could learn patterns in data without explicit labels. This opened new avenues for applications in fields like **natural language processing**.

Despite these impressive advancements, early neural networks were not without their challenges. Limited computational resources and lack of large datasets hindered progress, and the vanishing gradient problem was a significant obstacle. However, these hurdles were stepping stones that paved the way for the rapid advancement of neural network research and applications we see today.

Applications And Successes in Various Fields

Machine learning, has transformed numerous industries over the past few years. Its capability to learn from data and improve over time has made it an invaluable tool in various fields. In this section, we will explore some notable applications and successes of machine learning across different domains, highlighting how it has changed the way we work and live.

Healthcare

One of the most notable applications is in *medical imaging*. Algorithms can analyze images from MRIs, CT scans, and X-rays to detect diseases, such as cancer, with remarkable accuracy. For instance, a study published in "Nature" demonstrated that a machine learning model outperformed radiologists in diagnosing breast cancer from mammograms[45].

Another application is **predictive analytics**. Hospitals use machine learning to predict patient admissions and readmissions. By analyzing historical patient data, hospitals can allocate resources more efficiently. For example, Mount Sinai Health System in New York implemented a machine learning model that reduced readmission rates by 20%, ultimately improving patient care[46].

Finance

The finance sector has also seen tremendous success with machine learning. *Credit scoring* is one area where these algorithms excel. Traditional credit scoring models often rely on limited data, whereas machine learning can analyze a broader range of factors, including consumer behavior and transaction history. This enables financial institutions to make more informed lending decisions.

Fraud detection is another important application. Banks and credit card companies use machine learning to identify unusual patterns in transactions that may indicate fraud. For instance, PayPal uses machine learning algorithms to analyze millions of transactions per day, successfully reducing fraud rates by over 50%[47].

Retail

In retail, machine learning is revolutionizing the way businesses operate. One of the biggest applications is personalized marketing. Retailers use machine learning algorithms to analyze customer data and behaviors, enabling them to deliver tailored recommendations. Amazon, for example, has famously used machine learning to suggest products based on past purchases, significantly boosting sales[48].

Inventory management is another area where machine learning shines. Companies like Walmart use predictive analytics to forecast demand and optimize stock levels[49]. This not only reduces waste but also ensures that customers find the products they want when they shop.

Transportation

The transportation industry has also benefited greatly from machine learning, particularly with the advent of autonomous vehicles. Companies like Waymo and Tesla are leveraging machine learning to develop self-driving car technology[50]. These vehicles use data from sensors and cameras to learn how to navigate roads safely.

Additionally, ride-sharing services such as Uber and Lyft employ machine learning for dynamic pricing and route optimization. By analyzing real-time data, these companies can adjust prices based on demand and suggest the quickest routes for drivers, improving efficiency and customer satisfaction.

Agriculture

Farmers are using machine learning algorithms to analyze data from sensors deployed in fields. This helps them monitor crop health, predict yields, and optimize irrigation. For example, the company Blue River Technology uses machine learning to develop "See & Spray" technology that can distinguish between crops and weeds, allowing for more precise herbicide application[51].

Machine learning assists in precision agriculture, where farmers use data analytics to optimize planting and harvesting. By analyzing weather patterns and soil conditions, they can make informed decisions that lead to higher productivity and lower costs.

FIELD	APPLICATION	SUCCESS EXAMPLE
Healthcare	Medical Imaging	ML outperformed radiologists in breast cancer detection
Finance	Credit Scoring	Improved lending decisions using diverse data
Retail	Personalized Marketing	Amazon's product recommendations boost sales
Transportation	Autonomous Vehicles	Waymo's self-driving technology
Agriculture	Crop Monitoring	Blue River Technology's precision herbicide application

The applications and successes of machine learning in various fields have been remarkable. From healthcare to finance, retail, transportation, and agriculture, machine learning has not only improved efficiencies but has also enhanced the quality of services provided. As technology continues to evolve, we can expect even more innovative applications that will further shape our world.

CHAPTER 4
The Big Data Revolution

The term **"Big Data"** started surfacing in the late 1990s, but the foundations were laid much earlier. In the 1960s and 1970s, when computers began to evolve, data was mostly stored on physical media like *tapes* and *disks*. Businesses and researchers began to recognize that collecting and analyzing data could provide valuable insights, but the technology available at the time was limited. Data collection was not as streamlined, and the ability to analyze large datasets effectively remained a challenge[52].

In the 1980s and 1990s, the rise of personal computing initiated a cultural shift. More individuals and organizations began using computers, leading to an explosion in data generation. Companies started to accumulate customer information, sales data, and operational metrics. However, most businesses were still struggling with how to store and analyze this growing amount of information. Traditional database systems could not keep up with the increasing data volume, variety, and velocity.

The real turning point came in the early 2000s. The internet underwent rapid growth, and social media platforms began to emerge. Websites generated massive amounts of data daily, ranging from user interactions to content sharing. This data was no longer limited to structured formats like spreadsheets; it now included unstructured data from social media posts, videos, and images. The need for more advanced data management solutions became evident.

In 2001, *Doug Laney*, an analyst at Gartner, introduced the "3 Vs" concept of **Big Data: Volume, Variety, and Velocity**[53]. Volume refers to the sheer amount of data being generated, Variety highlights the different types of data, and Velocity emphasizes the speed at which data is created and processed. These principles helped organizations understand the challenges posed by Big Data, paving the way for new strategies and technologies.

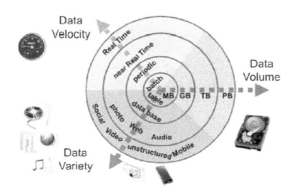

One significant milestone in the Big Data revolution was the introduction of **Hadoop** in 2005. Developed by *Doug Cutting* and *Mike Cafarella*, Hadoop is an open-source framework that allows for the distributed processing of large datasets across clusters of computers. This system enabled organizations to store vast amounts of data and analyze it more efficiently than ever before[54].

The rise of cloud computing in the late 2000s further accelerated the Big Data movement. **Cloud platforms** allowed businesses to scale their data storage and processing capabilities without significant upfront investments in hardware. Companies could now analyze their data in real-time, gaining insights that were previously impossible due to technological constraints.

By the 2010s, organizations across various sectors began leveraging Big Data in innovative ways. Industries like retail, healthcare, and finance started incorporating data analytics into their decision-making processes, leading to improved efficiencies and outcomes. The advent of machine learning and AI technologies also coincided with this period, as more data allowed for more robust algorithms and models.

Today, Big Data continues to evolve, and its impact on AI is profound. As we move forward in this book, we will explore how this vast amount of data is not just transforming industries but also reshaping our understanding of intelligence itself.

YEAR	MILESTONE	DETAIL
1960s-70s	Early Data Collection	Initial steps in data storage and analysis.
1980s-90s	Rise of Personal Computing	Increased data generation from personal use.
2001	Introduction of "3 Vs"	Doug Laney's framework for understanding Big Data.
2005	Launch of Hadoop	Open-source framework for processing large datasets.
Late 2000s	Growth of Cloud Computing	Scalability in data storage and processing.
2010s	Integration of Big Data and AI	Businesses leverage data analytics for decision-making.

Importance of Big Data: How the Availability of Large Datasets Transformed AI

Big data influence is evident in the way AI systems are developed, trained, and implemented across various industries. The availability of large datasets has allowed AI developers to create more sophisticated, efficient, and accurate models.

One of the primary ways big data has transformed AI is through the ability to **train machine learning models more effectively**. In the past, AI systems were limited by the quantity and quality of data available for training. With large datasets, AI algorithms can learn from a broader range of examples. This diversity enables the models to recognize patterns and make predictions with higher precision.

Consider the difference between training a model on a small dataset of a few hundred images versus one that contains millions of images. The larger dataset allows the model to see various scenarios, objects, and contexts. This exposure **helps the AI system generalize better**, meaning it can adapt to new, unseen data more effectively. This is particularly important in fields like image recognition, where the nuances between similar objects can be subtle.

Furthermore, the size of the dataset **directly correlates to the accuracy of AI models**. Larger datasets provide a more comprehensive understanding of the task at hand, reducing the margin for error. For instance, in natural language processing (NLP), having access to vast amounts of text data enables AI systems to grasp the complexities of human language better. They can learn grammar, context, idioms, and even cultural references, resulting in more natural and relevant interactions.

The importance of big data is also evident in its ability to support continuous learning. **AI models can be updated and retrained as new data** becomes available, which is essential for maintaining relevance in our fast-paced world. For example, businesses that rely on customer feedback can continuously improve their AI systems by analyzing new reviews and comments. This ongoing process helps to refine the AI's understanding and responsiveness to customer needs.

Additionally, big data facilitates **improved decision-making**. In sectors such as healthcare, finance, and retail, AI can analyze vast amounts of data to identify trends, make recommendations, and predict outcomes. For example, in healthcare, AI systems can sift through millions of patient records to identify potential treatment plans that have proven effective for similar cases. This data-driven approach enhances the quality of care and speeds up the diagnostic process.

Moreover, big data **aids in risk assessment and management**. In finance, algorithms analyze market patterns and consumer behavior to make informed predictions about investment opportunities or potential risks. This capability allows organizations to make decisions based on solid evidence rather than intuition alone, ultimately leading to better outcomes.

The relationship between big data and AI is a continuous cycle. As AI systems become more advanced, they generate even more data, which, in turn, can be leveraged for further development. This synergy has made it possible to tackle complex problems across various domains, from climate modeling to personalized marketing strategies.

The availability of large datasets has fundamentally transformed artificial intelligence. By enhancing training processes, improving model accuracy, and supporting informed decision-making, big data has paved the way for more effective and intelligent AI systems.

Technological Advancements: Developments in Storage and Processing Power

In recent years, the field of big data has experienced remarkable technological advancements that have significantly enhanced both storage and processing capabilities. These improvements not only support the growing volume of data but also enable faster and more efficient analysis. Below are some key developments in storage solutions and processing power, shedding light on how these advancements impact the world of artificial intelligence.

Storage Solutions

The first major area of advancement in big data technologies is storage. Traditional methods of data storage struggled to keep up with the exponential growth of data generated by various sources. Here are some significant developments in this area:

1. **Cloud Storage:** The rise of cloud computing has revolutionized how data is stored and accessed. Services like Amazon S3, Google Cloud Storage, and Microsoft Azure allow businesses to store massive amounts of data without the need for physical servers. This not

only reduces costs but also offers scalability. Companies can easily increase their storage capacity as their data needs grow[55].

2. **Distributed File Systems:** Technologies like Hadoop Distributed File System (HDFS) have made it possible to store data across multiple servers[56]. This approach not only enhances data availability but also increases redundancy and fault tolerance. If one server fails, the data remains accessible from another server, ensuring business continuity.

3. **Data Lakes:** Unlike traditional databases that require data to be structured before storage, data lakes allow storage of vast amounts of raw, unprocessed data[57]. This flexibility enables organizations to store data in its native format and process it later as needed. As a result, businesses can analyze data from various sources without spending time on initial data structuring.

4. **Solid-State Drives (SSDs):** The shift from traditional Hard Disk Drives (HDDs) to SSDs has greatly improved the speed of data retrieval and storage. SSDs offer significantly faster read and write speeds, which accelerates the time it takes to access data for processing. As prices for SSD technology continue to decline, more organizations are adopting them for their data storage needs[58].

Processing Power

Alongside advancements in storage, processing power has also seen significant improvements. The ability to quickly analyze large datasets is crucial for deriving insights and making informed decisions. Here are some noteworthy advancements:

1. **Multi-Core Processors:** Modern processors often come with multiple cores, allowing them to perform several operations simultaneously. This parallel processing capability speeds up data analysis tasks, making it feasible to work with large datasets in real-time[59].

2. **Graphics Processing Units (GPUs):** Initially designed for rendering graphics in video games, GPUs have found their way into data processing. Their architecture allows for high levels of parallelism, making them ideal for tasks such as machine learning and deep learning. As a result, using GPUs can exponentially reduce the time needed for training machine learning models[60].

3. **In-Memory Computing:** This technology allows data to be stored in the main memory (RAM) instead of on traditional disk storage. By doing so, organizations can access and process data

significantly faster. Platforms like Apache Ignite and SAP HANA utilize in-memory computing to facilitate real-time analytics, enabling quicker decision-making[61].

4. **Quantum Computing:** Although still in its infancy, quantum computing holds immense potential for big data processing. Quantum bits (qubits) can represent multiple states simultaneously, allowing quantum computers to solve complex problems at speeds unattainable by classical computers[62]. As this technology matures, it could revolutionize data processing and analysis capabilities.

The continuous advancements in storage and processing power are crucial for harnessing the full potential of big data. With innovations like cloud storage, distributed systems, and in-memory computing, organizations can now manage and analyze vast amounts of data more efficiently than ever before. These developments create an environment where artificial intelligence can thrive, leading to better insights and improved decision-making.

Case Studies: Successful AI Applications Driven by Big Data

According to a CNN report, although there is no precise figure for the amount of data within Big Data, it is estimated that over 90% of all existing data was created just last year—and this figure is continually rising. This sheer volume of data, however, is essentially useless in its raw form. This is where AI steps in, making sense of the data and driving innovation across various sectors[63].

Coca-Cola: Quenching Thirsts with Data

Coca-Cola, a global beverage leader, is a prime example of how big data and AI can drive business success. With an expansive portfolio of over 500 brands sold in more than 200 countries, Coca-Cola generates a staggering amount of data every day. This data comes from various segments of its operations—sourcing, production, distribution, sales, and customer feedback.

The company has invested significantly in AI to sift through this vast data pool and extract actionable insights. By analyzing consumer trends, Coca-Cola can tweak its offerings based on regional preferences for flavors, packaging, and healthier options. This targeted approach not only meets consumer demands but also streamlines production and supply chain processes.

With 35 million Twitter followers and 105 million Facebook fans, the brand taps into AI-driven image recognition technology to monitor when and where its drinks are being consumed and shared online. This data is invaluable for understanding demographics and consumer motivations, allowing Coca-Cola to deploy ads that are four times more likely to be clicked than standard advertisements.

By integrating AI and big data analytics into its strategic decisions, Coca-Cola continues to innovate. From its Freestyle soda fountain machines to digital engagement platforms, the company is well-positioned to maintain its competitive edge in a dynamic market.

Starbucks: Brewing Success with Personalization

Starbucks, with its massive global presence and 90 million transactions a week, stands as a beacon of big data and AI success in the retail sector. The coffee giant has effectively used these tools to revolutionize its marketing and sales strategies.

Central to Starbucks' data strategy is its loyalty card program and mobile app. These platforms capture detailed purchase data from millions of customers. Through AI and business intelligence (BI) tools, Starbucks leverages this data to predict customer preferences and send personalized offers via app notifications and emails. This level of customization encourages repeat visits, driving sales and enhancing customer loyalty.

The insights gained from big data also allow Starbucks to send tailored offers and discounts. These go beyond standard promotions, using individual purchase histories to craft messages that resonate with each customer. For instance, a customer who hasn't visited in a while might receive a personalized email with a tempting offer to lure them back.

Starbucks' ability to personalize its marketing efforts has not only increased foot traffic but also boosted customer satisfaction. By understanding and anticipating consumer needs, Starbucks ensures its place at the forefront of the coffee retail industry.

Elsevier: Revolutionizing Information Accessibility

Elsevier, a global leader in scientific and medical publishing, has been at the forefront of using AI and big data to enhance its operations. With over 140 years of history, the company has amassed a vast repository of data. The digital revolution prompted Elsevier to transition from traditional paper-based publications to digitized literature, opening up a new world of possibilities—and challenges.

One of the main hurdles was information overload. With global data doubling every two years, filtering valuable information became crucial. Elsevier turned to AI and big data to solve this problem. By analyzing the reading habits of its users, Elsevier could identify which types of content were most consumed. This insight allowed the company to use machine learning algorithms to tailor information delivery, ensuring readers received relevant and actionable data.

The result was a streamlined access to crucial information, enhancing the user experience and reinforcing Elsevier's status as a leader in scientific publishing. This approach not only improved user satisfaction but also ensured that researchers and practitioners received timely and pertinent information.

Veri-Flix: Battling Fake News with AI

In an era where misinformation can spread at unprecedented speeds, the fight against fake news has become paramount. Veri-Flix, a Belgian startup, is at the frontline of this battle, using AI and Big Data to authenticate news content. Supported by Google funding, Veri-Flix has developed a sophisticated system that employs machine learning to scrutinize user-generated videos.

The process begins with the collection of metadata such as video content, timestamps, and geolocation. By comparing this data across multiple uploads, Veri-Flix can assess the credibility of the news. This innovative use of AI has not only garnered recognition but also practical application, as evidenced by its adoption by Belgium's largest media station.

The technology's success lies in its ability to identify discrepancies and provide a reliable source of truth amidst a sea of misinformation. Veri-Flix's approach embodies the potential of AI and Big Data to foster accountability and trust in media.

Transforming Healthcare with Predictive Analytics

Healthcare systems worldwide grapple with the challenge of aligning staffing levels with fluctuating patient numbers. In Paris, four hospitals have tackled this issue head-on by integrating AI and big data into their operational strategies. This initiative has not only minimized wait times but also improved the quality of care delivered to patients.

The approach begins with the use of an open-source AI analytics platform that processes a decade's worth of admission data. By incorporating additional datasets like flu patterns, weather conditions, and public holidays, the hospitals can accurately predict patient admission rates up to two weeks in advance. This foresight allows hospital administrators to adjust staffing levels proactively, ensuring that resources are allocated efficiently during peak times.

Additionally, this predictive capability extends beyond mere staffing adjustments. The insights gleaned from these data analyses help in forecasting the demand for various services, thereby reducing wastage and streamlining healthcare delivery. This model serves as a beacon of innovation, demonstrating how data-driven decision-making can revolutionize patient care.

Pioneering Autonomous Maritime Transport

While autonomous automobiles have captured the public's imagination, the maritime industry is quietly undergoing its own transformation. A collaboration between Google and Rolls-Royce is spearheading the development of autonomous ships, leveraging AI and big data to navigate complex maritime environments.

The core of this initiative lies in the use of machine learning algorithms, akin to those employed by Google for voice and image recognition. These algorithms are trained to identify and classify objects encountered at sea, assessing the potential hazards they pose. The training process is augmented by vast datasets sourced from sensors and cameras mounted on vessels.

What sets this project apart is its real-time data sharing capability, facilitated by cloud-based AI applications. This enables seamless communication between ships and on-shore control centers, ensuring that navigational decisions are informed by the latest data. The implications of this technology are profound, promising enhanced safety and efficiency in maritime logistics.

CHAPTER 5
Deep Learning and Neural Networks

Basics of Deep Learning and Neural Networks

Within AI, machine learning acts as a subset focused on the ability of machines to improve from experience without being explicitly programmed. Delving deeper, **deep learning** is a subfield of machine learning. The defining characteristic of deep learning is its use of neural networks with multiple layers—hence the term *"deep.[64]"*

Deep learning excels over traditional machine learning by automating the feature extraction process. Instead of requiring humans to identify the most relevant data features, deep learning models can discern these features themselves, given enough data. This capability makes deep learning particularly suited for working with unstructured data, like text and images, which constitutes more than 80% of data within organizations.

Neural networks, drawing inspiration from the human brain, consist of nodes (or neurons) that process input data and pass it through interconnected layers to produce an outcome. The depth of these layers is what distinguishes regular neural networks from deep learning models[65].

1. **Input Layer:** This is where the raw data enters the neural network. Each node in this layer represents a feature or attribute of the data. For example, if you are processing images, each pixel could be a node in the input layer.

2. **Hidden Layers:** These layers are where the computation occurs. A neural network can have one or more hidden layers, with each layer containing multiple nodes. The nodes in these layers

receive input from the previous layer, apply a certain transformation, and pass their output to the next layer. The more hidden layers a network has, the "deeper" it is.

3. **Output Layer:** This layer produces the final output of the neural network. Depending on the task, it could be a single value (like in regression tasks) or multiple values (like in classification tasks).

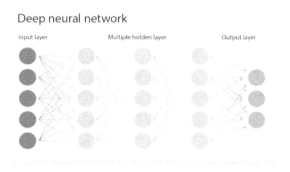

Most deep neural networks operate in a feed-forward manner, meaning data flows in one direction—from input to output. However, training these models involves a process called **backpropagation**. During backpropagation, the model adjusts its weights by moving backward from output to input, correcting errors to improve accuracy.

Enterprises leverage deep learning for tasks that require sophisticated pattern recognition. For instance, virtual assistants like *Siri* or *Alexa* use deep learning to understand and process human language. Similarly, deep learning is instrumental in fraud detection by identifying anomalies in transaction patterns.

A deep learning model's ability to cluster inputs based on observed patterns is one of its most powerful features. For example, it can categorize images of pizzas, burgers, and tacos by recognizing similarities and differences—tasks that are challenging for traditional machine learning models due to their simpler data structures.

Key Innovations of Deep Learning and Neural Networks

The innovations of CNNs, RNNs, and Transformers have revolutionized how we approach complex data types in deep learning. Each architecture brings unique strengths and capabilities, making them suitable for a wide array of applications. As artificial intelligence continues to evolve, understanding these key innovations will be essential for harnessing the power of deep learning in various fields.

Convolutional Neural Networks (CNNs)

Convolutional Neural Networks are a type of deep learning model specifically designed to analyze and interpret visual data. Unlike traditional neural networks that treat input data as a flat array, CNNs consider the spatial structure of images. This means they can recognize patterns and features in images more effectively, allowing them to identify objects, faces, or even complex scenes with a high degree of accuracy. They have transformed how we approach tasks such as image recognition, video analysis, and even medical image diagnostics.

CNN's design is a structure that mimics how humans and animals perceive visual information. This architecture consists of multiple layers, each responsible for extracting different features from an image. Here's the primary components that make up a CNN[66]:

1. **Convolutional Layers:** These are the essential building blocks of CNNs. They apply filters to the input image to create feature maps. These filters slide over the image to detect patterns such as edges, textures, or specific shapes. The number of filters can vary, allowing the model to learn and recognize a wide range of features.

2. **Activation Functions:** After the convolution operation, an activation function is applied to introduce non-linearity into the model. The most common activation function used in CNNs is the Rectified Linear Unit (ReLU). It helps the network learn complex patterns by allowing it to consider only positive values.

3. **Pooling Layers:** Once features are extracted, pooling layers reduce the dimensionality of the feature maps. This process helps to summarize the information while retaining the most critical features. Max pooling, which selects the maximum value from a group of values, is often used.

4. **Fully Connected Layers:** After several convolutional and pooling layers, the neural network connects to fully connected layers. Here, the model combines all the extracted features to make a final prediction, such as identifying an object in an image.

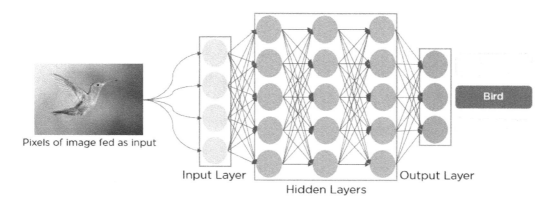

SOURCE: https://www.analyticsvidhya.com/blog/2021/05/convolutional-neural-networks-cnn/

CNNs have several advantages that make them a preferred choice for image-related tasks:

1. **Automatic Feature Extraction:** Unlike traditional machine learning models that require manual feature extraction, CNNs automatically learn the most relevant features during the training process. This capability significantly reduces the time and effort needed to prepare data for analysis.

2. **Translation Invariance**: CNNs are designed to recognize objects regardless of their position in an image. This means that whether an object is in the center or corner of an image, the model can still identify it accurately.

3. **Reduced Parameters:** Because of shared weights in convolutional layers, CNNs have fewer parameters compared to fully connected networks. This reduction helps prevent overfitting and allows the model to generalize better to new data.

The impact of CNNs can be seen across various domains:

1. **Image Recognition:** CNNs are widely used in applications such as facial recognition, where they analyze images to identify individuals.

2. **Medical Imaging:** In healthcare, CNNs assist in diagnosing diseases by analyzing medical images such as X-rays and MRIs.

3. **Self-Driving Cars:** CNNs also enables autonomous vehicles to interpret visual information from their surroundings, identifying pedestrians, road signs, and other vehicles.

Recurrent Neural Networks (RNNs)

RNNs are a class of neural networks designed to recognize patterns in sequences of data. This makes them particularly powerful for tasks where the context and order of information matter, such as language processing, time series analysis, and speech recognition. Traditional neural networks, known as feedforward networks, process inputs independently. They take a fixed-size input and produce a fixed-size output[67].

However, many real-world problems involve sequences of data where the order is important. For example, in natural language processing, the meaning of a word often depends on the words that come before or after it. RNNs have a unique architecture that allows them to maintain a form of memory. They achieve this through loops in their network connections, which enable them to remember previous information while processing new inputs. Because of this ability, RNNs can handle sequences of varying lengths, making them versatile for numerous applications.

At a basic level, an RNN processes data in a loop, where the output from the previous step is fed back into the network as input for the current step. This architecture allows the network to maintain a hidden state that carries information from previous inputs. Let's break this down further:

1. **Input Sequence:** The RNN receives a sequence of data points, one at a time.
2. **Hidden State:** After processing each data point, the RNN updates its hidden state, which encapsulates information from all previous inputs.
3. **Output:** After processing the entire sequence, the RNN produces an output, which might be a prediction, classification, or another form of data.

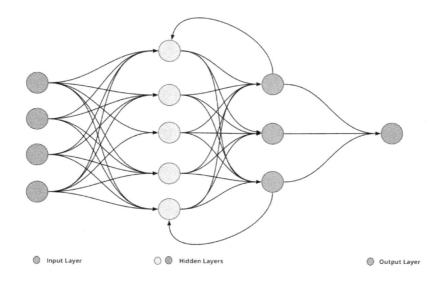

SOURCE: *https://i0.wp.com/dataaspirant.com/wp-content/uploads/2020/11/3-Recurrent-Neural-Network.png*

RNNs are used in a variety of fields and applications:

1. **Natural Language Processing**: RNNs excel at tasks like language translation and sentiment analysis, where understanding the context of words is crucial.

2. **Speech Recognition:** They can learn and predict patterns in audio signals, making them useful for voice-activated systems.

3. **Time Series Forecasting:** RNNs can analyze data collected over time, such as stock prices or weather patterns, to make predictions about future values.

While RNNs are powerful, they are not without their challenges. One major issue is the problem of vanishing and exploding gradients. During training, the gradients that are used to update the weights of the network can become too small or too large, making it difficult for the network to learn long-range dependencies in the data.

To address these limitations, more advanced architectures, such as Long Short-Term Memory (LSTM) networks and Gated Recurrent Units (GRUs), have been developed. These architectures introduce mechanisms that allow the network to better retain important information for longer periods.

Transformers

Transformers were first introduced in a paper titled "Attention is All You Need" by Vaswani et al. in 2017[68]. This architecture moved away from traditional recurrent neural networks (RNNs) and convolutional neural networks (CNNs) that dominated the field. Instead, Transformers rely on a mechanism called attention, which allows the model to weigh the importance of different words in a sentence, regardless of their position. This ability to focus on relevant parts of the input has proven to be extremely effective in understanding complex relationships in data.

The architecture of transformers consists of an encoder and a decoder. The encoder processes the input data and compresses it into a set of continuous representations, while the decoder uses these representations to generate output. Let's break down the key components:

1. **Self-Attention Mechanism:** This allows the model to consider the relationships between all words in a sentence simultaneously. Each word's representation is adjusted based on its connection to other words, enabling a deeper understanding of context.

2. **Multi-Head Attention:** Instead of having a single attention mechanism, Transformers utilize multiple attention heads. This means the model can learn different representations of the same input simultaneously, capturing various aspects of the data.

3. **Positional Encoding:** Since Transformers do not inherently understand the order of words (unlike RNNs), they use positional encoding to retain the sequence information. This encoding helps the model grasp the order of words in a sentence, which is crucial for understanding meaning.

4. **Feed-Forward Neural Networks:** After the attention layers, Transformers include feed-forward networks that process the representations further. These networks apply additional transformations to enhance the model's capability to learn complex patterns.

5. **Residual Connections and Layer Normalization:** To improve training efficiency and stability, Transformers implement residual connections around each sub-layer and apply layer normalization. This helps in maintaining the flow of gradients, making it easier to train deeper networks.

Transformers have found applications in various fields, primarily in natural language processing. Some notable uses include:

1. **Machine Translation:** Services like Google Translate have adopted Transformer-based models to improve translation accuracy.

2. **Text Summarization:** Transformers can efficiently condense large texts into shorter summaries while retaining essential information.

3. **Chatbots and Virtual Assistants**: AI-driven chatbots leverage Transformers to understand user queries and respond appropriately.

NEURAL NETWORK TYPE	MAIN FEATURES	TYPICAL APPLICATIONS
Convolutional Neural Networks (CNNs)	Convolutional layers, pooling layers, fully connected layers	Image classification, medical imaging, object detection
Recurrent Neural Networks (RNNs)	Memory retention, backpropagation through time	Natural language processing, speech recognition, time series analysis
Transformers	Self-attention mechanism, positional encoding, parallel processing	Machine translation, text summarization, large language models

Impact and Application on Various Industries

Deep learning and neural networks reshaping various industries by providing innovative solutions to some of the most pressing challenges. In this section, we will explore the impact and application of deep learning and neural networks across different sectors, highlighting their benefits and real-world uses.

Healthcare

The healthcare industry has seen significant advancements with the introduction of deep learning. By leveraging large datasets and sophisticated algorithms, healthcare providers are enhancing patient care, diagnosis, and treatment planning. Here are some notable applications:

1. **Medical Imaging:** Deep learning models, particularly convolutional neural networks (CNNs), are widely used for analyzing medical images such as X-rays, MRIs, and CT scans. These models can identify abnormalities, tumors, or fractures with high accuracy. For example, a study published in "Nature" found that a deep learning algorithm was able to match or exceed the performance of human radiologists in detecting breast cancer[69].

2. **Predictive Analytics:** Deep learning algorithms can analyze patient data to predict health outcomes. Predictive models can forecast the likelihood of diseases such as diabetes or heart conditions by examining factors like age, weight, and lifestyle choices. By using these models, healthcare providers can identify at-risk patients and intervene early.

3. **Drug Discovery:** Deep learning is also revolutionizing the drug discovery process. Traditional methods can be time-consuming and expensive, but deep learning helps to streamline this process. Algorithms can analyze vast chemical databases to identify potential drug candidates more quickly. For instance, researchers at Atomwise have used deep learning to predict the effectiveness of compounds against diseases like Ebola, speeding up the initial screening process[70].

4. **Personalized Medicine:** Deep learning enables healthcare providers to offer personalized treatment plans. By analyzing genomic data and patient histories, these algorithms can help tailor therapies to individual patients, improving treatment efficacy and reducing side effects. This approach is particularly beneficial in oncology, where the genetic makeup of tumors can significantly impact treatment options.

Finance

The finance industry is another area where deep learning and neural networks are making a significant impact. Financial institutions are utilizing these technologies to enhance decision-making, improve customer service, and manage risks more effectively. Here are some key applications:

1. **Fraud Detection:** Deep learning models are highly effective at detecting fraudulent transactions. By analyzing patterns in transaction data, these algorithms can identify anomalies that may indicate fraud. For instance, companies like PayPal and Mastercard use deep learning to monitor transactions in real-time, significantly reducing fraud losses[71].

2. **Algorithmic Trading:** Hedge funds and investment firms are increasingly adopting deep learning for algorithmic trading. These algorithms analyze market data and identify trading opportunities much faster than human traders. They can process vast amounts of information, including news articles, social media sentiment, and historical trading patterns, to make informed trading decisions.

3. **Credit Scoring:** Deep learning enhances credit scoring models by incorporating a wider range of data sources. Traditional credit scoring relies on limited information, but deep learning models can consider alternative data, such as social media activity or online behavior, to assess creditworthiness. This approach helps lenders make more accurate lending decisions and expand access to credit for individuals who may be overlooked by traditional methods.

4. **Customer Service**: Financial institutions are using deep learning for customer service through chatbots and virtual assistants. These AI-driven tools can understand natural language and respond to customer inquiries 24/7. By analyzing customer interactions and feedback, these systems continually improve their responses, enhancing customer satisfaction and reducing operational costs.

Retail

In the retail sector, deep learning and neural networks are being utilized to enhance customer experiences, optimize inventory management, and improve sales forecasting. Here are some key applications:

1. **Personalized Recommendations:** Retailers like Amazon and Netflix use deep learning algorithms to analyze customer behavior and purchase history. This analysis enables them to offer personalized product recommendations. According to a report by McKinsey, personalized recommendations can increase sales by up to 30%[72].

2. **Customer Sentiment Analysis:** Retailers use natural language processing (NLP), a component of deep learning, to analyze customer reviews and feedback. By understanding customer sentiments, companies can improve their products and services. A study by Deloitte found that businesses that engage with customers based on sentiment analysis see a 10-15% increase in customer satisfaction[73].

3. **Inventory Management:** Deep learning helps retailers optimize their stock levels by predicting demand more accurately. For example, Walmart employs advanced neural networks to analyze sales data and weather patterns to determine which products to stock and when. This results in reduced excess inventory and fewer stockouts, ultimately improving profitability.

4. **Visual Search:** Companies like Pinterest and ASOS have integrated visual search capabilities powered by deep learning. Shoppers can upload images to find similar products, making the

shopping experience more intuitive. Reports indicate that visual search can lead to higher conversion rates, as customers can find what they want faster.

Transportation

The transportation industry has also embraced deep learning and neural networks to enhance safety, efficiency, and productivity. Here are some notable applications:

1. **Autonomous Vehicles:** Companies like Tesla and Waymo are at the forefront of developing self-driving cars using deep learning. Neural networks process vast amounts of data from sensors and cameras, allowing vehicles to navigate roads safely. According to Statista, the global autonomous vehicle market is expected to reach over $2.3 trillion by 2030[74].

2. **Predictive Maintenance:** Airlines and logistics companies utilize deep learning to predict equipment failures before they occur. By analyzing data from various sensors, neural networks can identify patterns indicative of potential issues. A report by Accenture estimates that predictive maintenance can reduce maintenance costs by up to 30% and improve operational efficiency[75].

3. **Traffic Management:** Cities are using deep learning to optimize traffic flow and reduce congestion. For instance, traffic lights can be adjusted in real-time based on data from cameras and sensors, leading to smoother traffic patterns. Research indicates that smart traffic management can reduce travel times by 20-30%[76].

4. **Route Optimization:** Delivery companies like UPS and FedEx leverage deep learning algorithms to optimize delivery routes. By analyzing factors such as traffic, weather, and delivery times, these companies can reduce fuel consumption and improve delivery efficiency. According to UPS, their route optimization efforts have saved over 10 million gallons of fuel annually[77].

Deep learning and neural networks are changing the way industries operate by providing innovative solutions to complex problems. As these technologies continue to evolve, their applications will likely expand, offering even more opportunities for efficiency, accuracy, and improvement across various sectors. Understanding their impact can empower businesses to harness the power of AI and stay ahead in an increasingly competitive landscape.

CHAPTER 6
Current Trends and Breakthroughs

Natural Language Processing (NLP)

Natural Language Processing, often abbreviated as NLP focuses on the interaction between computers and humans through natural language. It allows machines to understand, interpret, and respond to human language in a way that is both meaningful and useful. The goal of NLP is to enable computers to process human language in the same way that humans do, making communication with machines more intuitive and efficient[78].

NLP has become a vital component of many applications we encounter daily. From voice-activated assistants like Siri and Alexa to chatbots that assist us on websites, NLP enhances the way we interact with technology. Understanding how NLP works can offer insight into its significance and its growing role in our lives.

Key Components of NLP

1. **Tokenization:** This is the first step in processing text. Tokenization involves breaking down a string of text into smaller units such as words or phrases. For example, the sentence "Natural Language Processing is fascinating" would be split into the tokens: "Natural," "Language," "Processing," "is," and "fascinating."

2. **Part-of-Speech Tagging**: After tokenization, the next step is to identify the part of speech for each token. This means determining whether a word is a noun, verb, adjective, etc. This helps the computer understand the grammatical structure of a sentence.

3. **Named Entity Recognition (NER):** This component identifies and classifies key elements in text, such as names of people, organizations, locations, dates, and other specific terms. For example, in the sentence "Apple Inc. was founded by Steve Jobs," NER would identify "Apple Inc." as an organization and "Steve Jobs" as a person.

4. **Sentiment Analysis:** This process involves determining the emotional tone behind a series of words. For instance, understanding whether a piece of text expresses positive, negative, or neutral sentiments can be particularly useful for businesses monitoring customer feedback.

5. **Parsing:** Parsing breaks down sentences into their components and shows how they relate to one another. This structural analysis helps in understanding the meaning of sentences more deeply.

6. **Text Summarization:** This is the process of condensing a large body of text into its main points. NLP can automatically generate summaries which can save time for readers and provide quick insights.

7. **Machine Translation:** This is the automatic translation of text from one language to another, such as Google Translate. It requires a deep understanding of both the source and target languages to deliver accurate translations.

While NLP has come a long way, it still faces several challenges. Language is nuanced and complex, which can lead to misunderstandings. For example, sarcasm and idiomatic expressions often confuse machines. Additionally, the variability in language across different cultures and contexts can present obstacles for NLP systems.

As technology continues to evolve, so does the potential of NLP. Researchers are constantly working on improving algorithms and models to enhance understanding and processing. The future may hold even more advanced capabilities that allow for more natural and fluid interactions between humans and machines.

Application of NLP

As our world becomes increasingly digital, the applications of NLP are expanding, making conversations between humans and machines more seamless. Let's explore some of the key applications of NLP and how they are transforming various industries.

1. **Sentiment Analysis**: Sentiment analysis is the process of determining the emotional tone behind a series of words. Businesses use this technique to gauge customer opinions on their products or services by analyzing social media posts, reviews, and surveys. By applying NLP algorithms, companies can classify sentiments as positive, negative, or neutral, helping them make informed decisions based on customer feedback. This not only assists in improving products but also enhances customer satisfaction.

Positive: "I love this product!"

Negative: "This is the worst!"

Neutral: "It's okay."

2. **Chatbots and Virtual Assistants**: Chatbots provide immediate assistance to users without the need for human intervention. Using NLP, these virtual assistants can understand user queries and respond appropriately, improving the customer experience. They can handle a wide range of inquiries, from FAQs to troubleshooting, making them an invaluable asset for businesses looking to enhance their customer support.

3. **Language Translation:** NLP also breaks down language barriers through machine translation. Applications like Google Translate utilize NLP techniques to convert text from one language to another, making information accessible to people around the globe. This is particularly beneficial in our interconnected world, where communication across different languages is essential for business, travel, and cultural exchange.

4. **Text Summarization**: In an era where information overload is a common challenge, text summarization tools powered by NLP can help distill lengthy documents into concise summaries. These tools analyze the main ideas and provide a brief overview, making it easier for individuals to grasp essential information without spending hours reading. This application is valuable for students, professionals, and anyone who needs to process large volumes of information quickly.

5. **Speech Recognition**: Popular applications like Apple's Siri and Google Assistant rely on this technology to understand voice commands and respond accurately. This not only enhances user convenience but also opens doors for individuals with disabilities, allowing them to interact with technology in more accessible ways.

6. **Content Recommendation**: Streaming platforms, news websites, and social media platforms use NLP to analyze user preferences and behavior. By understanding the language and context of users' interactions, these systems can suggest relevant content, improving user engagement and satisfaction. For instance, Netflix recommends shows based on your viewing history, making it easier for you to find something you'll enjoy.

Developments In Language Models of NLP

Language models are systems that use statistical methods to predict the next word in a sentence. Early models relied on simple techniques, such as n-grams, which considered only a limited number of preceding words. These models struggled with understanding context and often produced incoherent sentences. However, with the introduction of deep learning, researchers began to develop more complex models that could consider larger contexts and learn from vast amounts of text data.

BERT: Bidirectional Encoder Representations from Transformers

Introduced by Google in 2018, BERT revolutionized the way NLP tasks are approached. Unlike previous models that read text in a left-to-right or right-to-left direction, BERT uses a bidirectional approach. This means it considers the context of a word based on all the other words in a sentence, rather than just the ones that precede or follow it[79].

Key Features of BERT:

1. **Contextual Understanding:** By analyzing words in context, BERT can better understand the meaning of sentences. This is particularly useful for tasks like sentiment analysis or question answering.
2. **Fine-Tuning:** BERT can be fine-tuned for specific tasks with relatively small datasets. This process involves taking the pre-trained model and adjusting it to perform well on a specific problem, such as identifying spam emails or classifying customer feedback.
3. **Wide Adoption**: Since its release, BERT has been widely adopted in various applications, from search engines to chatbots, improving their performance and making them more effective at understanding human language.

T5: Text-to-Text Transfer Transformer

Introduced by Google Research in 2019, T5 represents a shift in how we approach NLP tasks. Instead of treating each task—like translation, summarization, or question answering—as separate aspects, T5 reframes every NLP problem as a text-to-text problem. This means that input and output are always in text form, allowing for a more unified approach to various tasks[80].

Key Features of T5:

1. **Unified Framework:** By treating all tasks as text generation, T5 simplifies the training process. You can input a prompt like "Translate English to Spanish: Hello, how are you?" and receive the text output "Hola, ¿cómo estás?" This consistency streamlines the model's ability to learn from diverse tasks.

2. **Pre-training and Fine-tuning:** T5 utilizes a two-step process of pre-training and fine-tuning. During pre-training, it learns from a large dataset of diverse texts, allowing it to understand context, semantics, and grammar. Fine-tuning tailors the model to specific tasks, enhancing its performance in real-world applications.

3. **Scalability:** T5 comes in various sizes, allowing users to choose a model that fits their computational resources and application needs. This flexibility makes it accessible for businesses of all sizes.

T5 has achieved state-of-the-art results across several NLP benchmarks. It outperformed previous models in tasks such as summarization, translation, and question answering. Due to its effectiveness in handling multiple tasks within a single framework, T5 has gained traction among researchers and developers looking for efficient solutions.

GPT-3: Generative Pre-trained Transformer 3

Launched by OpenAI in 2020, GPT-3 is one of the most powerful language models available today. With 175 billion parameters, it significantly surpasses its predecessor, GPT-2, which had only 1.5 billion parameters. The sheer size of GPT-3 enables it to generate coherent and contextually relevant text across a variety of topics[81].

Key Features of GPT-3:

1. **Text Generation:** GPT-3 excels at generating human-like text. Given a prompt, it can produce paragraphs, articles, or even poetry that is often indistinguishable from writing done by humans.

2. **Few-Shot Learning:** One of the standout capabilities of GPT-3 is its ability to perform a task with minimal examples, known as few-shot learning. Users can provide just a few examples, and GPT-3 can generalize from this small amount of information to generate relevant responses.

3. **Versatility:** GPT-3 can be used for various applications, including content creation, programming help, translation, and even generating creative writing. This versatility is a game-changer for industries that rely on content generation and customer interaction.

GPT-4: The Next Evolution

Following the remarkable success of GPT-3, OpenAI introduced GPT-4, which builds upon its predecessor with several enhancements. Released in March 2023, GPT-4 has gained attention for its improved capabilities, making it a powerful tool for developers and businesses[82].

Key Features of GPT-4:

1. **Broader Knowledge Base:** GPT-4 has access to a more extensive dataset than GPT-3, incorporating more recent information. This broader knowledge base allows it to generate more accurate responses and stay relevant in rapidly changing fields.

2. **Better Context Handling:** While GPT-3 was already impressive, GPT-4 takes context handling to the next level. It can consider longer inputs, allowing for more coherent and contextually relevant outputs. This improvement is particularly important for complex conversations and multi-turn interactions.

3. **Enhanced Safety and Alignment:** GPT-4 incorporates advanced safety features to minimize harmful and biased outputs. OpenAI has put significant effort into ensuring that the model aligns better with user intent, making its use more ethical and responsible.

GPT-4 has demonstrated remarkable performance across a variety of tasks, including creative writing, coding, and more. It outperforms GPT-3 in several benchmarks, making it a valuable asset for businesses looking to leverage AI in content creation, customer support, and other applications.

MODEL	YEAR RELEASED	KEY FEATURES
BERT	2018	Bidirectional context, excels in understanding nuances in language
T5	2019	Text-to-text framework, versatile across tasks
GPT-3	2020	175 billion parameters, few-shot learning, highly capable text generation
GPT-4	2023	Improved reasoning and instruction-following, enhanced coherence

AI In Robotics: Advances In Autonomous Systems and Robotics

Autonomous systems are machines designed to operate independently, with minimal human intervention. They can perceive their environment, make decisions, and execute actions based on those decisions. A key component in this process is machine learning, which allows robots to learn from data and improve their performance over time[83].

Perception and Navigation

AI equips robots with the ability to interpret sensory data and navigate through their environments effectively. Perception involves processing inputs from sensors like cameras, LIDAR, and ultrasonic sensors. These inputs help robots form a coherent understanding of their surroundings.

Using computer vision, powered by machine learning, robots can recognize objects and obstacles. This includes identifying various objects and even interpreting human gestures, allowing for more natural interactions. In navigation, AI-driven systems use algorithms for path planning, obstacle avoidance, and adapting to environmental changes. Techniques such as *simultaneous localization and mapping (SLAM) enable* robots to build and update maps while tracking their positions. For example, AI-powered robots in warehouses navigate narrow aisles, avoiding obstacles like pallets and other robots.

Object Identification

Object identification is crucial for robots to recognize and classify items accurately. This capability is vital for tasks from industrial automation to personal assistance. AI techniques, primarily through computer vision, allow robots to analyze visual data using deep learning models like Convolutional Neural Networks (CNNs). These models, trained on vast datasets, extract features from images to identify objects, discerning shapes, textures, and colors.

This technology is exemplified in autonomous shopping systems that identify a wide array of products. AI's role in object identification enhances robotic functionality, enabling sophisticated interactions and decision-making. As AI technology progresses, object identification continues to improve, unlocking new possibilities for intelligent systems.

Collision Avoidance

Collision avoidance is essential in ensuring robots can navigate safely without colliding with obstacles. This process combines perception, decision-making, and control mechanisms, powered by AI and sensor technologies. Robots use sensors like LIDAR and cameras to detect and map their surroundings, providing real-time data on obstacles and terrain. AI models process this data to create dynamic environmental maps.

Decision-making algorithms analyze these maps to predict potential collisions, using path planning and trajectory optimization to calculate safe routes. When an obstacle is detected, the system can recalibrate its route or slow down. Control systems then adjust the robot's speed and direction to navigate safely. Advanced AI models can predict the movement of dynamic obstacles, like people or other robots, adapting in real time. Collision avoidance is crucial across various applications, from precision agriculture to medical robotics.

Multimodal Large Language Models

Multimodal Large Language Models (LLMs) are revolutionizing AI in robotics by enabling machines to process diverse inputs, such as text, images, and audio. Unlike traditional models that rely on a single input type, multimodal LLMs provide richer context and more intelligent decision-making.

In healthcare, robots use multimodal LLMs to assist in diagnostics by analyzing medical images, patient data, and textual reports simultaneously for more accurate results. In autonomous systems, these models enhance situational awareness by combining visual data, sensor information, and real-time traffic updates to make informed decisions. As multimodal LLMs evolve, they expand the scope of tasks robots can perform, integrating diverse inputs to create more adaptive and intelligent systems.

AI's integration into robotics is transforming the capabilities of autonomous systems. Through advancements in perception and navigation, object identification, collision avoidance, and multimodal LLMs, robots are becoming more efficient, safe, and functional. These technologies promise to redefine the landscape of automation and intelligent systems, paving the way for a future where robots play an integral role in various sectors.

AI FUNCTION	DETAIL	EXAMPLE
Perception & Navigation	Interpret sensory data and navigate environments	Warehouse robots avoiding obstacles
Object Identification	Recognize and classify items	Autonomous shopping systems identifying products
Collision Avoidance	Navigate safely without collisions	Medical robots in complex environments
Multimodal LLMs	Process diverse inputs for richer decision-making	Healthcare diagnostics using multiple data types

Applications of AI in Robotics

The applications of AI in robotics are vast and varied. With AI at the core of these advancements, robots are transforming how we work, live, and explore new horizons. Here are some sectors where these technologies are making a difference[83]:

1. **Autonomous Vehicles**: In the automotive sector, this is epitomized by self-driving cars. These vehicles use AI to process data from sensors like LiDAR and cameras, enabling them to understand road conditions, detect obstacles, and make real-time decisions to ensure safe driving. Similarly, AI-powered drones automate flight tasks, allowing them to survey areas and deliver goods independently. In warehouses, AI helps robots streamline logistics by mapping routes and avoiding obstacles efficiently.

2. **Healthcare Robotics**: AI-powered robots are revolutionizing healthcare, from surgery to patient care. Robotic-assisted surgeries, such as those using the Da Vinci system, enhance precision in minimally invasive procedures. AI guides surgical instruments with remarkable accuracy, reducing human error and improving patient recovery times.

Beyond surgery, AI-driven robots assist in rehabilitation and elder care, tracking patient vitals, delivering medication, and providing companionship. This integration of AI in healthcare robotics enables more personalized and efficient care, easing the burden on healthcare systems.

3. **Manufacturing and Automation**: AI's role in manufacturing and automation has redefined production processes, making them more efficient and adaptable. AI-powered robots perform tasks ranging from assembly to quality control with unmatched speed and precision. Machine learning

allows these robots to optimize operations by learning from data. Predictive maintenance, facilitated by AI, anticipates machine malfunctions, reducing downtime and costs. Collaborative robots, or cobots, work alongside humans safely, enhancing productivity and workplace safety through precise, repetitive tasks.

4. **Agriculture**: In agriculture, AI has led to increased efficiency and crop yields. AI-powered robots handle tasks like planting, harvesting, and monitoring crops, reducing manual labor. These robots analyze soil conditions, predict weather patterns, and identify crop diseases, enabling data-driven decisions that optimize resource use.

Robotic harvesters pick fruits and vegetables with precision, minimizing crop damage. Drones equipped with AI monitor fields, detecting crop health issues and applying treatments only where needed, promoting sustainable farming practices. Thus, AI in agriculture helps meet global food demands while minimizing environmental impact.

5. **Space Exploration**: AI is crucial in space exploration, where autonomous robots operate in challenging environments. These robots use machine learning to navigate planetary surfaces, collect data, and make decisions based on surroundings.

For example, NASA's Perseverance rover on Mars uses AI to select rock samples for analysis without constant input from mission control. AI processes the vast data collected, aiding scientists in quicker and more accurate analyses. In spacecraft, AI optimizes mission planning, navigation, and fuel usage, making long-duration space missions more feasible and efficient.

AI's integration into robotics spans diverse fields, enhancing capabilities and efficiency. From autonomous vehicles to space exploration, AI-driven robots are transforming industries and opening new possibilities.

Recent AI Advancements in Robotics

The field of robotics is undergoing a rapid transformation, thanks to recent advancements in artificial intelligence. These developments are making robots more intelligent, autonomous, and adaptable, enabling them to handle complex tasks with greater efficiency. Let's explores some of the most impactful AI advancements in robotics, focusing on machine learning, computer vision, natural language processing, and the integration of AI with vision systems[83].

Advanced Machine Learning Models

These models, particularly deep learning and neural networks, allow robots to process vast amounts of data and recognize complex patterns. This capability is crucial for tasks such as object detection, facial recognition, and predictive maintenance.

Reinforcement learning, a subset of machine learning, plays a pivotal role in enhancing the adaptability of robots. By learning from trial and error, robots can refine their performance and adapt to new situations over time. This adaptability is essential for robots operating in dynamic environments, such as autonomous vehicles and service robots that interact with diverse user needs. As a result, advanced machine learning models are driving the evolution of robotics, making machines more intelligent and capable of handling real-world tasks.

Enhanced Computer Vision

Advancements in computer vision have transformed how robots perceive and interact with their environment. AI-powered visual systems enable robots to perform real-time object recognition, scene analysis, and depth perception with remarkable accuracy. These capabilities are essential for a wide range of applications, from autonomous vehicles and drones to manufacturing robots and healthcare devices.

In industrial settings, computer vision helps robots inspect products, detect defects, and ensure quality control. The integration of advanced image processing techniques and neural networks allows robots to interpret visual data more effectively. Enhanced computer vision is thus a cornerstone of modern robotics, enabling more sophisticated and autonomous machines.

Natural Language Processing (NLP)

NLP technologies, such as those used in Amazon's Alexa and Apple's Siri, have improved our ability to interact with machines, making these interactions more natural and intuitive. Modern NLP technologies enable robots to understand and respond to spoken language with greater accuracy and contextual awareness.

Sophisticated algorithms analyze syntax, semantics, and context, allowing robots to engage in meaningful conversations. Additionally, NLP advancements support multilingual capabilities, enabling robots to interact with users in various languages. This progress enhances the usability of service robots and conversational agents, making interactions smoother and more efficient. NLP is crucial for developing robots that can understand and communicate with humans in a user-friendly manner.

The Integration of Vision and AI

AI and camera modules work together to automate various tasks, and advancements in sensor technology have enabled camera modules to capture high-quality images for AI models. In AI-enabled robotic applications, accuracy is paramount, as image analysis and interpretation often require a high level of detail. Cameras play a crucial role in ensuring that robots can complete their tasks accurately and without errors.

ADVANCEMENT	IMPACT ON ROBOTICS
Machine Learning Models	Enhanced decision-making, adaptability, and task handling
Computer Vision	Real-time object recognition, scene analysis, and accuracy
Natural Language Processing	Improved human-robot interaction and multilingual support
Vision and AI Integration	High-quality image capture and accurate task completion

Ethical Considerations: AI Ethics, Bias, and Responsible AI

The increasing reliance on AI systems raises significant concerns about fairness, accountability, and transparency. First and foremost, the ethical implications of AI affect everyone. As these technologies are implemented into critical systems, the possibility of unintended consequences skyrockets. For example, AI algorithms used in hiring processes can inadvertently replicate existing biases, leading to unfair treatment of candidates based on gender, race, or socioeconomic status. Addressing these ethical considerations ensures that AI serves as a tool for empowerment rather than oppression.

Moreover, the decisions made by AI systems can have real-world consequences. A healthcare AI that misdiagnoses a patient due to biased data can lead to serious health risks. Similarly, AI used in law enforcement may perpetuate systemic biases if trained on historical data that reflects discriminatory practices. By focusing on ethical AI, we can work to mitigate harm and foster systems that prioritize human well-being.

AI ethics is a framework that addresses the moral implications and responsibilities associated with the development and deployment of AI technologies. This framework helps ensure that AI systems work for the benefit of society while minimizing harm. Some core principles of AI ethics include:

1. **Fairness:** AI systems should treat all individuals and groups equitably, avoiding discrimination based on race, gender, age, or other characteristics.
2. **Transparency:** The processes and decisions made by AI systems should be understandable to users. Transparency builds trust and helps ensure accountability for AI-driven decisions.
3. **Accountability:** Developers and organizations should be responsible for the outcomes of their AI systems. They must establish clear guidelines for who holds accountability in case of negative consequences.
4. **Privacy:** Data used by AI systems should be handled with care. Protecting users' personal information is vital in maintaining trust and ensuring compliance with legal standards.

The Issue of Bias in AI

One of the most pressing issues in AI ethics is bias. AI systems can unintentionally perpetuate or amplify existing biases found in training data. For example, if a facial recognition system is trained primarily on images of people from a specific demographic, it may perform poorly on individuals from other demographics. This can lead to unfair treatment in applications such as hiring, lending, and law enforcement.

APPLICATION	TYPE OF BIAS	IMPACT
Facial Recognition	Racial and Gender Bias	Higher error rates for non-white and female faces
Hiring Algorithms	Gender Bias	Disproportionate rejection of female candidates
Predictive Policing	Racial Bias	Over-policing in minority communities
Credit Scoring	Socioeconomic Bias	Disadvantaging lower-income applicants

To combat bias in AI systems, developers and organizations can adopt several strategies:

1. **Diverse Datasets:** Ensure that the training data includes a wide range of demographics and perspectives. This helps create a more balanced understanding of different groups.

2. **Regular Audits:** Conduct regular assessments of AI systems to identify and correct biases. This includes monitoring outcomes and adjusting algorithms as necessary.

3. **Inclusive Development Teams:** Build diverse teams to develop AI solutions. Different viewpoints can help identify potential biases that may not have been considered.

4. **Feedback Mechanisms:** Implement systems for users to provide feedback on AI decisions. This can help identify issues and foster improvements.

Responsible AI Development

Responsible AI focuses on creating systems that adhere to ethical principles and actively work to minimize harm. Here are several key principles that guide responsible AI practices:

1. **Human-Centric Design:** AI should be designed with the needs and rights of users in mind. Developers should consider how AI impacts individuals and communities and prioritize user well-being.

2. **Fairness and Non-Discrimination:** AI systems should be developed to promote fairness and avoid discrimination. This includes regularly evaluating algorithms for bias and ensuring equitable access to AI benefits.

3. **Transparency and Explainability:** It is essential to provide clear explanations of how AI systems work, particularly in high-stakes applications. Users should understand how decisions are made and have access to information about the underlying algorithms.

4. **Accountability and Governance:** Organizations that develop and deploy AI must establish clear accountability frameworks. This includes defining who is responsible for AI decisions and creating systems for oversight and redress.

5. **Continuous Monitoring and Improvement:** AI technologies should be continuously monitored for ethical compliance and performance. Organizations should be committed to ongoing evaluation and improvement of their AI systems.

CHAPTER 7
The Future of AI

Predictions And Speculations: Expert Opinions on The Future Trajectory Of AI

Artificial Intelligence (AI) is no longer a distant dream. It's here, and its influence stretches across nearly every industry. As we look to the future, experts anticipate AI will continue to evolve, impacting sectors like healthcare, education, finance, military, cybersecurity, transportation, and advertising in profound ways.

Healthcare: A Revolution in Patient Care

In healthcare, AI is poised to revolutionize how we diagnose and treat illnesses. In countries like India, where access to healthcare is limited due to a shortage of qualified professionals and infrastructure, AI can bridge the gap. It can analyze data from fitness trackers or medical histories to diagnose diseases and recommend treatments.

This not only empowers individuals but also enhances the healthcare industry's efficiency by leveraging vast amounts of data. AI's adaptability makes it an invaluable tool in this sector, promising a future where healthcare is more accessible and personalized.

Education: Tailoring Learning Experiences

The education sector is on the brink of transformation with AI. Traditional schooling may soon be a thing of the past, as AI offers personalized learning experiences tailored to individual needs. This could help students excel by focusing on their strengths and providing support where needed. AI in education holds the potential to create a more effective and inclusive learning environment, fostering a generation better equipped for the challenges of tomorrow.

Finance: Redefining Economic Strategies

AI's potential in finance is immense. Its ability to analyze vast amounts of data quickly and accurately is set to revolutionize investment strategies. AI-driven approaches could disrupt traditional trading and investment practices, making financial management more efficient and competitive. The rise of Robo-advisors and the integration of AI in financial decision-making are just the beginning. As AI continues to evolve, it will shape the future of finance, making it more accessible and efficient.

Military and Cybersecurity: Enhancing National Security

AI's role in military and cybersecurity is growing rapidly. Autonomous weapon systems and AI-assisted technologies offer a safer way to enhance national security. These technologies can execute missions with precision and efficiency, minimizing human risk. However, the challenge lies in ensuring these AI systems are explainable and reliable. As AI continues to develop, maintaining control and understanding of its decision-making processes will be crucial to avoid unintended consequences.

Transportation: Driving the Future

The transportation industry is already witnessing the impact of AI, with the advent of smart and autonomous vehicles. By 2025, it's expected that over 100% of vehicles will incorporate AI-driven technologies. These advancements promise safer and more efficient travel, with predictive systems alerting drivers to potential issues before they arise. The future of transportation is one where AI plays a central role, making travel more connected and intelligent.

Advertising: Precision in Marketing

AI is set to transform advertising by enabling campaigns that are more targeted and data-driven. AI systems can analyze historical data to predict campaign success, ensuring better returns on investment. This means businesses can market more effectively, reaching the right audiences with precision. The future of advertising lies in AI's ability to provide insights that drive smarter marketing decisions, ultimately leading to increased customer engagement and satisfaction.

The trajectory of AI is clear: it will continue to shape industries, making them more efficient, personalized, and data-driven. As we embrace this technology, understanding its potential and limitations will be key to harnessing its power responsibly.

Emerging AI Technologies

As artificial intelligence continues to evolve and integrate into various aspects of our lives, understanding these technologies can empower us to make informed decisions, enhance our productivity, and adapt to changes in our professional and personal environments.

They have the potential to reshape industries, from healthcare and finance to education and entertainment. Understanding how AI is changing the landscape can help individuals and businesses position themselves for success. Let's explore some of the most promising emerging AI technologies that are set to make a big impact[84].

Quantum Machine Learning: A Quantum Leap Forward

Quantum Machine Learning (QML) sits at the crossroads of quantum computing and machine learning. Imagine the computational power of quantum computers applied to the algorithms of machine learning. This combination opens doors to unprecedented processing capabilities.

At present, QML is largely in the theoretical realm, but early experiments are promising. Researchers are exploring how quantum algorithms can enhance machine learning processes. For instance, QML has shown potential in solving optimization problems more efficiently than classical methods. This capability is crucial in various fields, from logistics to drug discovery.

As quantum computers grow more powerful and accessible, the potential applications of QML are staggering. One of the most exciting prospects is its ability to provide exponential speedups in specific machine learning tasks. This capability could revolutionize fields like cryptography, where security relies on complex calculations, and financial modeling, which requires processing large datasets rapidly. Moreover, QML could transform complex system simulations, making it possible to model phenomena that are currently beyond our reach.

APPLICATION AREA	IMPACT
Cryptography	Enhanced security through complex algorithms
Financial Modeling	Faster data processing and analysis
Complex System Simulation	Improved accuracy and efficiency
Cryptography	Enhanced security through complex algorithms

Neuromorphic Computing: Mimicking the Brain

Neuromorphic computing aims to create computer hardware that mirrors the structure and function of biological neural networks. This approach could lead to AI systems that learn and adapt much like the human brain. Several neuromorphic chips have already been developed, demonstrating improved energy efficiency for specific AI tasks. These chips excel in processing tasks that traditional computers struggle with, such as pattern recognition and sensory data interpretation.

The future of neuromorphic computing holds the promise of enabling more powerful edge AI applications. For instance, it could facilitate real-time learning in robots, allowing them to adapt to new environments on the fly. Autonomous systems, such as self-driving cars, could benefit significantly from this technology, becoming more reliable and efficient.

Furthermore, neuromorphic computing might lead to a new era of AI that closely resembles biological intelligence, opening the door to machines that can understand and respond to the world in more human-like ways.

APPLICATION AREA	IMPACT
Edge AI Applications	Enhanced performance and efficiency
Robotics	Real-time learning and adaptability
Autonomous Systems	Improved reliability and decision-making

Advanced Neural Architectures and Generative Models

The recent evolution of neural network architectures has been nothing short of groundbreaking. Central to this revolution are transformer models, particularly Generative Pre-trained Transformers (like GPT), which have changed the landscape of natural language processing. Alongside these are Generative Adversarial Networks (GANs) and Diffusion Models, which are pushing the limits of what's possible in image and video generation.

These advanced models are making waves across various sectors. In content creation, they enable the generation of high-quality text, images, and videos, reducing the time and effort needed for creative processes. In customer service, they're powering chatbots that can understand and respond to queries with human-like fluency. Furthermore, in fields like drug discovery and scientific research, these models are accelerating the process of data analysis and hypothesis generation, making breakthroughs happen faster than ever before.

As these neural architectures continue to evolve, we can expect even more powerful AI systems. These systems will be capable of handling increasingly complex tasks across various domains, from personalized medicine to autonomous vehicles. The future of AI, driven by these technologies, will likely see machines that can learn and adapt in ways that were previously unattainable.

APPLICATION AREA	IMPACT
Content Creation	Enhanced efficiency and creativity
Customer Service	Improved interaction and responsiveness
Drug Discovery	Accelerated research and development

Federated Learning and Privacy-Preserving ML

As concerns over data privacy grow, Federated Learning has emerged as a game-changer. This technique trains AI models on distributed datasets without centralizing the data, allowing multiple parties to build a robust model collaboratively. Complementing this are privacy-preserving techniques like Differential Privacy and Homomorphic Encryption, which add layers of security to data processing and analysis.

These privacy-preserving technologies are already making a mark in sensitive domains such as healthcare and finance. They enable AI models to be trained on sensitive data without compromising individual privacy, thus facilitating secure collaboration in environments where data sharing was previously restricted by privacy concerns.

With global regulations tightening around data privacy, these technologies are set to become even more critical. They promise to enable AI applications in areas that were previously limited by privacy issues, fostering greater trust in AI systems. This, in turn, will open new avenues for cross-organizational and cross-border collaborations in AI development, paving the way for more holistic and inclusive innovation.

APPLICATION AREA	IMPACT
Healthcare	Secure data analysis and model training
Finance	Privacy-enhanced financial modeling
Cross-Border Collaboration	New opportunities for secure partnerships

Automated Machine Learning (AutoML) and Neural Architecture Search

AutoML is all about automating the machine learning process, making it easier and more efficient. It tackles tasks like feature selection, model selection, and hyperparameter tuning, which are traditionally time-consuming and require expert knowledge. Neural Architecture Search goes a step further by automating the design of neural network architectures, potentially leading to more efficient and powerful models.

AutoML tools are already democratizing access to machine learning. They allow non-experts to apply machine learning to real-world problems and enhance the efficiency of ML workflows. This accessibility is a game-changer, enabling more people and organizations to leverage AI technologies without the need for specialized knowledge.

As AutoML and Neural Architecture Search technologies mature, they could drastically accelerate AI research and development. They promise to democratize access to advanced AI capabilities, making cutting-edge technology available to a broader audience. Additionally, these technologies may lead to the discovery of novel neural architectures that outperform those designed by humans.

APPLICATION AREA	IMPACT
ML Accessibility	Broader access and application of AI
ML Workflow Efficiency	Enhanced efficiency and productivity
Novel Architecture Discovery	Potential for superior AI models

Societal Impact Of AI: Potential Impacts on Employment, Privacy, and Daily Life

Artificial Intelligence (AI) is rapidly becoming a staple in our daily routines, subtly reshaping the way we live, work, and interact. As we move forward, AI's influence promises to be both profound and pervasive, affecting nearly every aspect of society.

Employment: Redefining Jobs

AI is revolutionizing the workplace, bringing about both opportunities and challenges. On one hand, AI can enhance productivity and efficiency, automating routine tasks and freeing humans to focus on more complex, creative endeavors. However, this automation also raises concerns about job displacement. Many fear that as machines become more capable, they will replace human workers, leading to significant unemployment.

Yet, AI also creates jobs. New roles are emerging in AI development, maintenance, and oversight. Skills in data analysis, machine learning, and AI ethics are increasingly in demand. The key challenge for society is to ensure that workers are equipped with the skills needed to thrive in an AI-driven economy. Education and retraining programs will be crucial in this transition.

Privacy: A Looming Challenge

AI's impact on privacy is a pressing concern. As AI systems become more sophisticated, they can process vast amounts of personal data, often without explicit consent. This capability poses a threat to privacy, as AI can uncover intimate details about individuals, sometimes even more than we know about ourselves.

The erosion of privacy is not just a technological issue but an ethical one. Society must grapple with the balance between the benefits of AI and the right to privacy. As AI becomes more prevalent, establishing robust data protection frameworks will be essential to safeguard personal information. Regulations, such as the European Union's AI Act, aim to address these concerns, but the path forward is complex, with many legal and ethical challenges to navigate.

Daily Life: Increasing Tempo and Efficiency

AI is set to accelerate the pace of daily life. With AI-driven decision-making, businesses, governments, and other organizations can operate more efficiently, responding quickly to user needs and demands. This speed can enhance customer experiences, streamline operations, and drive innovation.

However, this increased tempo may also lead to stress and burnout as individuals strive to keep up with the rapid pace of change. Society will need to find ways to manage this acceleration, ensuring that the benefits of AI do not come at the expense of well-being.

Regulatory Environment

As AI becomes more entrenched in society, the legal landscape surrounding its use grows increasingly complex. Governments worldwide are racing to establish regulations that govern AI deployment. In the U.S., for instance, a patchwork of city, state, and federal laws is emerging, creating a challenging regulatory environment. Similarly, the European Union's AI Act aims to set a global standard for AI regulation, though its ultimate impact remains to be seen.

These regulatory efforts underscore the need for businesses and individuals to stay informed and compliant with evolving laws. As AI continues to advance, legal frameworks will need to adapt to ensure ethical use and address public concerns.

Despite concerns about AI replacing human roles, the concept of Human-AI teaming offers a hopeful alternative. This approach emphasizes collaboration, where AI augments human abilities rather than displacing them. By working alongside AI, individuals and organizations can leverage its strengths while retaining the human touch that machines cannot replicate.

Human-AI teaming can also help alleviate societal fears about AI. The portrayal of AI as a threat in popular culture has instilled deep-seated apprehension. By emphasizing collaboration, we can build trust in AI technologies, ensuring they are seen as tools that empower rather than threaten humanity.

Conclusion

As we reach the end of **"The Journey of Artificial Intelligence,"** let's take a moment to reflect on the path we've traveled. Throughout this book, we've explored the rich history of AI, witnessed its evolution, and glimpsed the exciting future that lies ahead.

We began by defining AI and understanding its significance in the modern world. From there, we traced the origins of AI, discovering the early mechanical inventions and pivotal contributions like those of Alan Turing. The landmark 1956 Dartmouth Conference marked the formal birth of AI as a field, setting the stage for decades of innovation.

In exploring the early days, we learned about symbolic AI and influential programs like the Logic Theorist and General Problem Solver. We also encountered the concept of the "AI Winter," periods when enthusiasm for AI waned, only to be revived by new breakthroughs.

The rise of machine learning marked a significant shift, moving from rule-based systems to statistical models. We delved into key algorithms and techniques, witnessing AI's increasing ability to learn from data and achieve remarkable successes across various fields.

The big data revolution transformed AI applications, thanks to the availability of large datasets and advancements in storage and processing power. We examined case studies from industries like healthcare and retail that have harnessed AI's potential to drive innovation and improve services.

Deep learning and neural networks came into focus, showcasing their impact across diverse industries such as healthcare, finance, and transportation. We explored the basics and key innovations, understanding how these technologies have pushed AI to new heights.

Current trends and breakthroughs in AI, including natural language processing and robotics, revealed the ongoing advancements shaping our world. We also discussed the ethical considerations surrounding AI, emphasizing the importance of responsible development.

Finally, we looked ahead to the future, exploring emerging AI technologies and their potential societal impacts. From quantum machine learning to privacy-preserving techniques, we discussed expert predictions and the challenges we must overcome to harness AI's full potential.

The journey of AI is a testament to human ingenuity and the relentless pursuit of understanding intelligence. From its humble beginnings to its current state, AI has evolved into a transformative force that touches every aspect of our lives. As we stand on the brink of new possibilities, it's clear that AI will continue to shape our world in profound ways.

However, as AI becomes more integrated into our daily lives, it's essential to address the ethical questions and challenges it presents. By fostering a culture of responsible development and thoughtful engagement, we can ensure that AI serves the greater good and contributes positively to society.

As we conclude this journey, I encourage you to stay informed and engaged with AI developments. The world of AI is dynamic and ever-changing, with new advancements happening at an unprecedented pace. By keeping yourself updated, you can make informed decisions about AI's role in your life and contribute to the ongoing conversation about its future.

Whether you're a tech enthusiast, a student, or simply curious about AI, your engagement matters. By understanding AI's history, present, and future, you become part of a larger community working towards a future where AI is used responsibly and ethically.

May your curiosity and passion for learning continue to guide you as we explore the endless possibilities of artificial intelligence together.

APPENDICES

GLOSSARY OF TERMS

1. **Algorithm:** An algorithm is a step-by-step set of instructions or rules designed to perform a specific task or solve a problem. In AI, algorithms are used to process data and generate predictions based on that data.

2. **Artificial Intelligence (AI):** AI refers to the simulation of human intelligence in machines programmed to think and learn like humans. This includes problem-solving, understanding language, and recognizing patterns.

3. **Artificial General Intelligence (AGI):** Artificial general intelligence refers to a type of AI that is capable of performing any intellectual task that a human can do. AGI is a theoretical concept that does not yet exist, as current AI systems are designed for specific tasks.

4. **Autonomous Systems:** Autonomous Systems are machines capable of performing tasks without human intervention. These systems use AI to navigate, make decisions, and learn from their environment, often seen in self-driving cars and drones.

5. **Bias:** In the context of AI, bias refers to systematic errors in data or algorithms that can lead to unfair outcomes. This can occur if the training data is not representative of the real-world population.

6. **Big Data:** Extremely large datasets that can be analyzed computationally to reveal patterns, trends, and associations. In AI, big data is crucial for training accurate models and improving their performance.

7. **Chatbot:** A chatbot is an AI program designed to simulate conversation with human users. Chatbots can be found in customer service applications, social media platforms, and other communication channels.

8. **Cognitive Computing:** Cognitive computing refers to systems that simulate human thought processes in complex situations. These systems can learn from data, understand natural language, and interact with users in a more human-like way.

9. **Computer Vision:** Computer vision is an area of AI that focuses on enabling machines to interpret and make decisions based on visual data from the world, such as images and videos. This technology is used in applications like facial recognition and autonomous vehicles.

10. **Data Mining:** The practice of examining large datasets to uncover hidden patterns, trends, and insights. In AI, data mining helps in extracting valuable information that can guide decision-making.

11. **Data Science:** Data science is an interdisciplinary field that combines statistics, computer science, and domain expertise to extract knowledge and insights from structured and unstructured data. It often overlaps with AI and machine learning.

12. **Deep Learning:** Deep learning is a specialized form of machine learning that uses neural networks with many layers (hence "deep") to analyze various factors of data. It is particularly effective for image and speech recognition.

13. **Ethics in AI:** Ethics in AI deals with the moral implications of using artificial intelligence. This includes considerations around privacy, fairness, accountability, and the societal impact of AI technologies.

14. **Explainable AI (XAI):** Explainable AI refers to methods and techniques that make the decision-making processes of AI systems transparent and understandable to humans. This is essential for building trust and ensuring accountability in AI applications.

15. **Expert System:** An expert system is a computer program that mimics the decision-making abilities of a human expert in a specific field. Expert systems use knowledge bases and inference rules to solve complex problems.

16. **Human-in-the-loop (HITL):** A design approach that incorporates human feedback in the AI decision-making process. HITL ensures that AI systems remain aligned with human values and can adapt to changing circumstances.

17. **Machine Learning (ML):** Machine learning is a subset of AI that focuses on teaching computers to learn from data and improve their performance over time without being explicitly programmed. It uses algorithms to identify patterns and make decisions based on input data.

18. **Model Evaluation:** Model evaluation is the process of assessing the performance of a machine learning model using various metrics. Common evaluation techniques include accuracy, precision, recall, and F1 score.

19. **Natural Language Processing (NLP):** NLP is a branch of AI that focuses on the interaction between computers and humans through natural language. It involves enabling machines to understand, interpret, and respond to human language in a valuable way.

20. **Neural Network:** A neural network is a computational model inspired by the human brain's structure. This system consists of layers of interconnected nodes (or "neurons") that process input data and produce output. Neural networks are fundamental to deep learning.

21. **Overfitting:** Overfitting occurs when a machine learning model performs well on training data but poorly on unseen data. This happens when the model learns noise or patterns that do not generalize beyond the training set.

22. **Predictive Analytics:** Predictive analytics involves using statistical algorithms and machine learning techniques to identify the likelihood of future outcomes based on historical data. This is widely used in business for decision-making.

23. **Reinforcement Learning:** Reinforcement learning is a type of machine learning where an agent learns to make decisions by taking actions in an environment to maximize some notion of cumulative reward. It is often used in robotics and game playing.

24. **Robotics:** Robotics is a branch of AI that deals with the design, construction, and operation of robots. It combines elements of engineering, computer science, and AI to create machines that can perform tasks autonomously or semi-autonomously.

25. **Supervised Learning:** Supervised learning is a type of machine learning where the model is trained on labeled data. This means that the input data comes with the correct output, allowing the model to learn and make predictions based on that information.

26. **Transfer Learning:** A machine learning technique where a model developed for one task is reused for a different, but related task. This can improve learning efficiency and performance on new tasks.

27. **Training Data:** Training data is the dataset used to train machine learning models. It provides the examples that the algorithm learns from, allowing it to make predictions or decisions.

28. **Underfitting:** Underfitting is the opposite of overfitting. It occurs when a model is too simple to capture the underlying trends in the data, resulting in poor performance on both the training and test datasets.

29. **Unsupervised Learning:** In contrast to supervised learning, unsupervised learning involves training a model on data without labeled responses. The model tries to identify patterns and relationships within the data on its own.

REFERENCES

1 Toomer, G. J. (2024, December 21). Archimedes | Facts & Biography. Encyclopedia Britannica. https://www.britannica.com/biography/Archimedes

2 Wikipedia contributors. (2024, December 12). Ismail Al-Jazari - Wikipedia. https://en.wikipedia.org/wiki/Ismail_al-Jazari

3 גולן, א. (n.d.). The Book of Knowledge of Ingenious Mechanical Devices. The Book of Knowledge of Ingenious Mechanical Devices. https://aljazaribook.com/en/page/2/

4 Wikipedia contributors. (2024b, December 12). History of the steam engine. Wikipedia. https://en.wikipedia.org/wiki/History_of_the_steam_engine

5 Wikipedia contributors. (2024a, December 10). Power loom. Wikipedia. https://en.wikipedia.org/wiki/Power_loom

6 Wikipedia contributors. (2024d, December 16). Boolean algebra. Wikipedia. https://en.wikipedia.org/wiki/Boolean_algebra

7 Wikipedia contributors. (2024a, October 1). Characteristica universalis. Wikipedia. https://en.wikipedia.org/wiki/Characteristica_universalis

8 Edmunds, M. (2024, December 18). Antikythera mechanism | Description, Purpose, & Facts. Encyclopedia Britannica. https://www.britannica.com/topic/Antikythera-mechanism

9 Nigel. (2022, September 30). Heron of Alexandria Steam engine. glue-it.com. https://www.glue-it.com/gallery/heron-of-alexandria-steam-engine/

10 Mechanical clock | Britannica. (n.d.). Encyclopedia Britannica. https://www.britannica.com/technology/mechanical-clock

11 The Editors of Encyclopaedia Britannica. (1999, May 4). Jacquard loom | Definition, HIstory, Computer, & Facts. Encyclopedia Britannica. https://www.britannica.com/technology/Jacquard-loom

12 Freiberger, P. A., & Swaine, M. R. (2024, December 18). Analytical Engine | Description & Facts. Encyclopedia Britannica. https://www.britannica.com/technology/Analytical-Engine

13 Copeland, B. (2024a, November 16). Alan Turing | Biography, Facts, Computer, Machine, Education, & Death. Encyclopedia Britannica. https://www.britannica.com/biography/Alan-Turing

14 Computing Machinery and Intelligence. (n.d.). Goodreads. https://www.goodreads.com/book/show/31381135

15 Team, I. (2024, August 5). The Turing Test: What is it, what can pass it, and limitations. Investopedia. https://www.investopedia.com/terms/t/turing-test.asp

16 Artificial intelligence (AI) coined at Dartmouth. (n.d.). Dartmouth. https://home.dartmouth.edu/about/artificial-intelligence-ai-coined-dartmouth

17 Wikipedia contributors. (2024b, December 8). John McCarthy (computer scientist). Wikipedia. https://en.wikipedia.org/wiki/John_McCarthy_(computer_scientist)

18 Wikipedia contributors. (2024g, December 24). Marvin Minsky. Wikipedia. https://en.wikipedia.org/wiki/Marvin_Minsky

19 Wikipedia contributors. (2024b, November 13). Nathaniel Rochester (computer scientist). Wikipedia. https://en.wikipedia.org/wiki/Nathaniel_Rochester_(computer_scientist)

20 Markowsky, G. (2024, December 2). Claude Shannon | Father of information theory, American engineer. Encyclopedia Britannica. https://www.britannica.com/biography/Claude-Shannon

21 Gugerty, L. (2006). Newell and Simon's Logic Theorist: Historical Background and Impact on Cognitive Modeling. Proceedings of the Human Factors and Ergonomics Society Annual Meeting, 50(9), 880–884. https://doi.org/10.1177/154193120605000904

22 Principia Mathematica (Stanford Encyclopedia of Philosophy). (2021, June 23). https://plato.stanford.edu/entries/principia-mathematica/

23 The Times of AI. (2023, August 15). The Roots of AI: General Problem Solver (GPS) (1957) [Video]. YouTube. https://www.youtube.com/watch?v=dww8eOj0fU0

24 Wikipedia contributors. (2024, November 28). Lisp (programming language). Wikipedia. https://en.wikipedia.org/wiki/Lisp_(programming_language)

25 Wikipedia contributors. (2024a, July 1). SHRDLU. Wikipedia. https://en.wikipedia.org/wiki/SHRDLU

26 Wikipedia contributors. (2024c, December 10). AI winter. Wikipedia. https://en.wikipedia.org/wiki/AI_winter

27 Wikipedia contributors. (2024c, December 9). Expert system. Wikipedia. https://en.wikipedia.org/wiki/Expert_system

28 Copeland, B. (2008, October 7). MYCIN | Expert System, Medical Diagnosis & Treatment. Encyclopedia Britannica. https://www.britannica.com/technology/MYCIN

29 Copeland, B. (2008a, October 7). DENDRAL | Artificial Intelligence, Machine Learning & Expert Systems. Encyclopedia Britannica. https://www.britannica.com/technology/DENDRAL

30 Wikipedia contributors. (2023, October 10). Xcon. Wikipedia. https://en.wikipedia.org/wiki/Xcon

31 Home | Prospector | Explore and Analyze global mining Projects. (n.d.). https://www.prospectorportal.com/

32 Wikipedia contributors. (2024e, December 20). CADUCEUS (expert system). Wikipedia. https://en.wikipedia.org/wiki/CADUCEUS_(expert_system)

33 Supervised Machine learning - Javatpoint. (n.d.). www.javatpoint.com. https://www.javatpoint.com/supervised-machine-learning

34 GeeksforGeeks. (2024, December 16). Linear Regression in Machine learning. GeeksforGeeks. https://www.geeksforgeeks.org/ml-linear-regression/

35 Parihar, G. (2021, December 14). Machine Learning: a journey from linear regression to logistic regression. Medium. https://medium.com/analytics-vidhya/machine-learning-a-journey-from-linear-regression-to-logistic-regression-741c4236e3cd

36 Upasana. (2020, November 25). Decision Tree: How to create a perfect decision tree? Edureka. https://www.edureka.co/blog/decision-trees/

37 Van Otten, N. (2024, November 15). Support Vector Machines (SVM) In Machine Learning Made Simple & How To Tutorial. Spot Intelligence. https://spotintelligence.com/2024/05/06/support-vector-machines-svm/

38 Wikipedia contributors. (2024c, November 29). Unsupervised learning. Wikipedia. https://en.wikipedia.org/wiki/Unsupervised_learning

39 Manglick, A. (2017, July 10). K-Means clustering. http://arun-aiml.blogspot.com/2017/07/k-means-clustering.html

40 GeeksforGeeks. (2024a, March 11). Hierarchical clustering in machine learning. GeeksforGeeks. https://www.geeksforgeeks.org/hierarchical-clustering/

41 Biswal, A. (2024, October 10). What is Principal Component Analysis (PCA) in ML? Simplilearn.com. https://www.simplilearn.com/tutorials/machine-learning-tutorial/principal-component-analysis

42 Wikipedia contributors. (2024h, December 30). Reinforcement learning. Wikipedia. https://en.wikipedia.org/wiki/Reinforcement_learning

43 Wikipedia contributors. (2024g, December 28). Neural network (machine learning). Wikipedia. https://en.wikipedia.org/wiki/Neural_network_(machine_learning)

44 Nath, S. (2023, August 30). From Perceptrons to Multi-Layered Networks: The Evolution of Neural Networks. Medium. https://medium.com/@sruthy.sn91/from-perceptrons-to-multi-layered-networks-the-evolution-of-neural-networks-c5d14c9bb1f9

45 Killock, D. (2020). AI outperforms radiologists in mammographic screening. Nature Reviews Clinical Oncology, 17(3), 134. https://doi.org/10.1038/s41571-020-0329-7

46 Shameer K, Johnson KW, Yahi A, Miotto R, Li LI, Ricks D, Jebakaran J, Kovatch P, Sengupta PP, Gelijns S, Moskovitz A, Darrow B, David DL, Kasarskis A, Tatonetti NP, Pinney S, Dudley JT. PREDICTIVE MODELING OF HOSPITAL READMISSION RATES USING ELECTRONIC MEDICAL RECORD-WIDE MACHINE LEARNING: A CASE-STUDY USING MOUNT SINAI HEART FAILURE COHORT. Pac Symp Biocomput. 2017;22:276-287. doi: 10.1142/9789813207813_0027. PMID: 27896982; PMCID: PMC5362124.

47 PayPal. (2024, November 6). Harnessing machine learning fraud detection technologies. PayPal. https://www.paypal.com/us/brc/article/payment-fraud-detection-machine-learning

48 Hardesty, L. (2024, November 14). The history of Amazon's recommendation algorithm - Amazon Science. Amazon Science. https://www.amazon.science/the-history-of-amazons-recommendation-algorithm

49 vorecol.com. (n.d.). How can companies effectively use data analytics for supply chain decisionmaking? https://vorecol.com/blogs/blog-how-can-companies-effectively-use-data-analytics-for-supply-chain-decisionmaking-74387

50 Song, J., Cho, Y. J., Kang, M. H., & Hwang, K. Y. (2020). An application of reinforced Learning-Based Dynamic Pricing for improvement of ridesharing platform service in Seoul. Electronics, 9(11), 1818. https://doi.org/10.3390/electronics9111818

[51] Blue River Technology: The field of Machine Learning - Digital innovation and transformation. (2021, April 19). Digital Innovation and Transformation. https://d3.harvard.edu/platform-digit/submission/blue-river-technology-the-field-of-machine-learning/

[52] Kumar, Y., Marchena, J., Awlla, A. H., Li, J. J., & Abdalla, H. B. (2024). The AI-Powered evolution of big data. Applied Sciences, 14(22), 10176. https://doi.org/10.3390/app142210176

[53] Ladani, V. a. P. B. D. (2014, April 21). Inner: Big Data – 3 Vs (volume, velocity and variety) and advantages. Technology and Web Security Stuffs. https://aboutdigitalcertificate.wordpress.com/2014/04/21/inner-big-data-3-vs-volume-velocity-and-variety-and-advantages/

[54] GeeksforGeeks. (2019b, January 18). Hadoop | History or Evolution. GeeksforGeeks. https://www.geeksforgeeks.org/hadoop-history-or-evolution/

[55] Wikipedia contributors. (2024d, December 5). Cloud storage. Wikipedia. https://en.wikipedia.org/wiki/Cloud_storage

[56] Yasar, K., Rosencrance, L., & Vaughan, J. (2024, April 19). Hadoop Distributed File System (HDFS). Search Data Management. https://www.techtarget.com/searchdatamanagement/definition/Hadoop-Distributed-File-System-HDFS

[57] Wikipedia contributors. (2024g, December 13). Data lake. Wikipedia. https://en.wikipedia.org/wiki/Data_lake

[58] Wikipedia contributors. (2024i, December 23). Solid-state drive. Wikipedia. https://en.wikipedia.org/wiki/Solid-state_drive

[59] Wikipedia contributors. (2024b, November 15). Multi-core processor. Wikipedia. https://en.wikipedia.org/wiki/Multi-core_processor

[60] Wikipedia contributors. (2024k, December 26). Graphics processing unit. Wikipedia. https://en.wikipedia.org/wiki/Graphics_processing_unit

[61] Admin, & Admin. (2022, June 28). In-Memory Computing: a Faster Method to Process Big Data - Alpha Numero. Alpha-Numero -. https://alpha-numero.com/in-memory-computing-a-faster-method-to-process-big-data/

[62] Wikipedia contributors. (2024k, December 24). Quantum computing. Wikipedia. https://en.wikipedia.org/wiki/Quantum_computing

[63] Great Learning. (2024, October 1). How artificial intelligence and big data together drive success – Top 5 case studies. Great Learning Blog: Free Resources What Matters to Shape Your Career! https://www.mygreatlearning.com/blog/ai-bigdata-case-study/

[64] Machine learning vs deep learning | Rudderstack. (n.d.). RudderStack. https://www.rudderstack.com/learn/machine-learning/machine-learning-vs-deep-learning/

[65] Nielsen, M. A. (2015). Neural networks and deep learning. http://neuralnetworksanddeeplearning.com/

[66] Wikipedia contributors. (2024i, December 18). Convolutional neural network. Wikipedia. https://en.wikipedia.org/wiki/Convolutional_neural_network

[67] Wikipedia contributors. (2024k, December 20). Recurrent neural network. Wikipedia. https://en.wikipedia.org/wiki/Recurrent_neural_network

[68] Wikipedia contributors. (2024f, December 29). Transformer (deep learning architecture). Wikipedia. https://en.wikipedia.org/wiki/Transformer_(deep_learning_architecture)

[69] Hickman, S. E., Baxter, G. C., & Gilbert, F. J. (2021). Adoption of artificial intelligence in breast imaging: evaluation, ethical constraints and limitations. British Journal of Cancer, 125(1), 15–22. https://doi.org/10.1038/s41416-021-01333-w

[70] Martin, G. (2016, July 13). This company uses AI to accelerate drug discovery. O'Reilly Media. https://www.oreilly.com/content/this-company-uses-ai-to-accelerate-drug-discovery/

[71] Tsymbal, T. (2024, December 3). Generative AI for Fraud Detection: Mechanisms & Real-World Examples. Master of Code Global. https://masterofcode.com/blog/generative-ai-for-fraud-detection

[72] vorecol.com. (n.d.-a). Emerging trends in personalization features for customer experience management. https://vorecol.com/blogs/blog-emerging-trends-in-personalization-features-for-customer-experience-management-167999

[73] vorecol.com. (n.d.-c). Leveraging AIPowered tools for enhanced customer engagement during economic uncertainty. https://vorecol.com/blogs/blog-leveraging-aipowered-tools-for-enhanced-customer-engagement-during-economic-uncertainty-166941

[74] Statista. (2024, December 25). Autonomous vehicle market size worldwide 2021-2030. https://www.statista.com/statistics/1224515/av-market-size-worldwide-forecast/

[75] Industrial internet of things offers significant opportunity for growth of digital services, says Accenture Report. (n.d.). https://newsroom.accenture.com/news/2014/industrial-internet-of-things-offers-significant-opportunity-for-growth-of-digital-services-says-accenture-report

[76] Dian, & Dian. (2024, October 11). Improving Road Safety with Smart Traffic in Saudi Cities. Saudi Arabia Transport and Mobility - Consulting Firm. https://saudimobilityconsulting.com/enhancing-road-safety-and-mobility-with-smart-traffic-systems/

[77] AI Case Study | UPS saves over 10 million gallons of fuel and up to $400m in costs annually with advanced telematics and analysis. (n.d.). Best Practice AI. https://www.bestpractice.ai/ai-case-study-best-practice/ups_saves_over_10_million_gallons_of_fuel_and_up_to_%24400m_in_costs_annually_with_advanced_telematics_and_analysis

[78] Gillis, A. S., Lutkevich, B., & Burns, E. (2024, August 28). What is natural language processing (NLP)? Search Enterprise AI. https://www.techtarget.com/searchenterpriseai/definition/natural-language-processing-NLP

[79] Wikipedia contributors. (2024q, December 30). BERT (language model). Wikipedia. https://en.wikipedia.org/wiki/BERT_(language_model)

[80] Wikipedia contributors. (2024q, December 30). BERT (language model). Wikipedia. https://en.wikipedia.org/wiki/BERT_(language_model)

[81] Wikipedia contributors. (2024f, December 8). GPT-3. Wikipedia. https://en.wikipedia.org/wiki/GPT-3

[82] Wikipedia contributors. (2024n, December 22). GPT-4. Wikipedia. https://en.wikipedia.org/wiki/GPT-4

[83] https://www.technexion.com/resources/applications-and-advancements-of-ai-in-robotics/

[84] The Future of Machine Learning: Predictions and speculations. (n.d.). https://gridlex.com/a/the-future-of-machine-learning-st6313

www.ingramcontent.com/pod-product-compliance
Lightning Source LLC
LaVergne TN
LVHW082128070326

832902LV00040B/2974